DJ KOOL HERC

COKE LA ROCK

DJ HOLLYWOOD

EDDIE CHEEBA

BLACK SPADES

RUSSELL SIMMONS

KURTIS BLOW

DJ RUN

DARRYL MCDANIELS

JAZZY DEE

RAHIEM

MR. NESS/ SCORPIO

KOOL DJ AJ

BUSY BEE STARSKI

LOVEBUG STARSKI

RODNEY C

JAZZY JEFF

BIG BANK HANK

WONDER MIKE

MASTER GEE

PAUL WINLEY

TANYA WINLEY

FATMAN

PUMPKIN

LARRY SMITH

HIP HOP FAMILY TREE

ED PISKOR

FANTAGRAPHICS BOOKS INC

HIP HOP FAMILY TREE

TABLE OF CONTENTS

THIS IS DEDICATED TO THE #!&&@$ THAT WAS DOWN FROM DAY ONE.

FANTAGRAPHICS BOOKS

7563 LAKE CITY WAY NE
SEATTLE, WASHINGTON 98115

EDITORIAL LIAISON: GARY GROTH
PRODUCTION: PAUL BARESH
DESIGN CONSULTATION: EMORY LIU
PUBLISHERS: GARY GROTH & KIM THOMPSON
ASSOCIATE PUBLISHER: ERIC REYNOLDS

SECOND FANTAGRAPHICS BOOKS EDITION: FEBRUARY 2014

ISBN 978-1-60699-690-4

PRINTED IN CHINA

IT'S THE MID-1970S, IN THE DILAPIDATED SOUTH **BRONX**. IF YOU'RE LOOKING FOR FUN, THE ONLY POSITIVE FORM OF RECREATION WOULD BE TO ATTEND ONE OF **DJ KOOL HERC'S** PARTIES, IN A REC ROOM LOCATED AT **1520 SEDGWICK AVE.**

HERC IS ALREADY A LEGEND IN THE BOROUGH, BUT THIS DOESN'T STOP HIM FROM CONSTANTLY PRACTICING AND EXPERIMENTING TO MAKE HIS SHOWS AS **ENJOYABLE** AS POSSIBLE.

PEOPLE BE GETTIN' **FUNKY** WHEN THIS DRUM BEAT TAKES OVER...

... BUT IT ONLY LASTS FOR A COUPLE SECONDS...

USING **2 COPIES** OF THE SAME **RECORD** HE DISCOVERS THAT HE CAN LOOP THE INSTRUMENTAL "**BREAKS**" IN HIS FAVORITE MUSIC **AD INFINITUM**, IF HE CHOOSES SO. TINKERING IN HIS APARTMENT WITH THE WINDOW OPEN, HE REALIZES HE'S ON TO **SOMETHING**...

MIXING ONE **BREAK** INTO THE BREAK OF A DIFFERENT SONG, A TERM HE CALLS "**MERRY-GO-ROUND**," BECOMES A PART OF **KOOL HERC'S** ARSENAL. ADDING SUCH **COMPLEXITY** TO HIS PERFORMANCE, HE MAKES THE DECISION TO ENLIST A FRIEND TO **EMCEE** AND HANDLE DUTIES ON THE **MICROPHONE**.

... COKE LA ROCK, AN' I AIN'T NO STEPPIN' STONE !!

BEING THE **ONLY** GAME IN TOWN, THESE PARTIES COMMAND **HUGE** CROWDS AND PROVIDE A **WEALTH** OF **INSPIRATION** TO THE **YOUNG** PEOPLE IN ATTENDANCE. A TALENTED **CORE** BEGINS TO BUILD UPON THE **FOUNDATION** THAT HERC DEVELOPS.

GRANDMASTER FLASH PERFECTS HERC'S MAJOR TECHNIQUES AND BEGINS INNOVATING NEW CONCEPTS AS HE GAINS POPULARITY PLAYING BLOCK PARTIES.

GRANDWIZARD THEODORE IS A YOUNG DJ* WHO INVENTS THE IDEA OF "**SCRATCHING**" RECORDS BY ACCIDENT.

TEDDY! TURN THAT NOISE DOWN!

?

ZIGGA ZIGGA

* MORE SPECIFICALLY, HE IS GRANDMASTER FLASH'S PROTÉGÉ.

AFRIKA BAMBAATAA IS A PARTY DJ, TOO, KNOWN FOR BEING AN ADVENTUROUS "**MASTER OF RECORDS**," BY PLAYING THE **WEIRDEST**, MOST **OBSCURE** MUSIC. HIS INCREDIBLY LOUD SOUND SYSTEM IS SECOND TO NONE.

GANG CULTURE IS RAMPANT IN THE BRONX AT THIS TIME. BAMBAATAA, HIMSELF, IS THE FEARED LEADER OF THE BIGGEST GANG IN THE BOROUGH.

SEEING THE POSITIVE POTENTIAL IN THIS NEW "HIP HOP" SCENE (CONSISTING OF BREAKDANCE, MC'S, DJ's, AND GRAFFITI ARTISTS), BAMBAATAA STARTS GUIDING HIS FOLLOWERS IN A LESS VIOLENT DIRECTION.

THIS INHERENT GANG VIBE MIGHT BE THE SOURCE OF WHY MOST OF THE CREATIVE PEOPLE DECIDE TO ESTABLISH GROUPS, RATHER THAN EXPRESS THEMSELVES ON THEIR OWN. THE "BATTLING" PHENOMENA, OF EACH HIP HOP DISCIPLINE IS CERTAINLY DERIVED FROM THE GANG MENTALITY.

THE TREACHEROUS THREE

THE COLD CRUSH BROTHERS

FUNKY FOUR PLUS ONE

THE FANTASTIC FIVE

AS THE **MUSIC** MAKES ITS WAY ACROSS TOWN, A QUEENS-BASED MC, **KURTIS BLOW**, IS A NOTABLE EXCEPTION TO THE GROUP/GANG PARADIGM. *

* BEING AN OPENING PERFORMER FOR **FLASH** DOES HIM GOOD.

HIS FRIEND/MANAGER, RUSSELL **"RUSH"** SIMMONS PLAYS A BIG PART IN BLOW'S SUCCESS.

IF WE GONNA MAKE YOU A BIGGAH THTAW THAN EDDIE CHEBA*, THEN YOU AIN'T KURT WALKAH NO MO'.

* EDDIE CHEBA IS ANOTHER SOLO MC, WITH DJ HOLLYWOOD.

CHEBA = MARIJUANA = CHEAP BLOW = COCAINE = HIGH CLASS... **PERCEPTION IS REALITY!!!**

TRUTHT ME. KURTITH BLOW ITH A HOT NAME!

IN P.T. BARNUM FASHION, **RUSH** HAS THE GENIUS IDEA TO UNITE HIS KID BROTHER, DJ **JOSEPH "RUN"** SIMMONS, AND KURTIS BLOW INTO A TANDEM ACT.

RUSSELL, MAN... I DON'T KNOW?

DON'T TRIP, KURTITH. THE KIDTH DEF!

THE **DUO** TAKES **QUEENS** BY **STORM!**

...LIKE A BULLET FROM A **GUN**. MY DISCO **SON**...

...COOL DJ RUN!

THEY SOON CATCH THE ATTENTION OF MORE PROFITABLE VENUES.

AW YOU THERIOTH? TALK TO ME WHEN YOU HAVE A REAL OFFAH.

A CAPITALIST FROM EARLY ON

THERE ARE WHISPERINGS THROUGHOUT **NEW YORK** ABOUT RECORDING HIP HOP MUSIC FOR MASS CONSUMPTION. THIS CAPTURES EVERYONE'S IMAGINATION, INCLUDING YOUNG **RUN**.

YO, RUSSELL! PUT ME ON REKKIDS, MAN!!

YEAH YEAH, GET A DEGREE FIRTHT THO YOU HAVE THUM'THIN' TO FALL BACK ON.

CHEBA

RUN SPRINTS TO TELL HIS HOMEBOY **DARRYL "GRANDMASTER GET HIGH" McDANIELS** WHAT RUSSELL SAID. McDANIELS SHARES A BOOK OF RHYMES THAT HE'S BEEN CULTIVATING.

YOU KNOW I'M BRINGING YOU IN THE STUDIO WIF ME, RIGHT?

WORD.

IT'S IMPORTANT TO RECOGNIZE **DJ HOLLYWOOD** AS BEING A CO-CREATOR OF HIP HOP. EVEN **BEFORE** KOOL HERC THREW HIS FIRST PARTY, HOLLYWOOD WAS THE **KING** OF THE UPSCALE, DOWNTOWN CLUBS. HE GETS LESS CREDIT FOR CREATING THE CULTURE, THOUGH, BECAUSE MOST FUTURE PARTICIPANTS WERE PRECLUDED FROM GOING DOWNTOWN TO SEE HOLLYWOOD DUE TO EXPENSIVE COVER CHARGES, FANCY DRESS CODES, AND STRICT AGE REQUIREMENTS.

BEST GIVE RESPECT! I CAME UP WITH THE TERM "HIP HOP."

ONE OF MANY TO MAKE THIS CLAIM.

HOLLYWOOD IS NO STRANGER TO THE MICRO-PHONE, BUT HIS EMCEE, **EDDIE CHEBA**, IS A **MASTER** OF CROWD PARTICIPATION.

...I'M LIKE THE HOT BUTTER ON YA BREAKFAST TOAST!

HOLLYWOOD AND CHEBA KNOW ABOUT WHAT'S HAPPENING IN THE PARKS AND IN THE REC ROOMS, BUT, THEY'RE MAKING TOO MUCH MONEY TO CARE. THEY DON'T SEE THE FEW, EXISTING, SOUTH BRONX DJ'S AS A THREAT.

THEY WOULDN'T EVEN BEGIN TO UNDERSTAND WHY THESE TWO KOOL HERC ACOLYTES, **DJ DISCO WIZ** AND **CASANOVA FLY**, WOULD DRAW POWER FROM A STREETLIGHT TO PLAY ON A BASKETBALL COURT FOR **FREE**.

SHOULD WE BUS' IT ON 'EM, **WIZ**?

BUS' IT!

WIZ AND CAZ ARE NOTORIOUS BATTLE DJ'S WHO HAVE THE INGENUITY TO PRESS THEIR OWN RECORD PLATE FULL OF CUSTOMIZED SOUND EFFECTS AND BREAKS.

IS Y'ALL READY FOR THE KNOCK-OUT PUNCH?!

THIS SECRET WEAPON ALMOST ALWAYS DESTROYS THEIR COMPETITION...

BU-BUMP SCREE BOMP BOMP BOOOOOOO~

"UPROCKING"

... TONIGHT, MORE THAN JUST THEIR RIVALS ARE TAKEN OUT.

?

...THE HELL?!

DID WE DO THAT SHIT?

ALL THE STREETLIGHTS IS OUT.

SOUNDS OF GLASS SMASHING CASCADE THROUGHOUT THE SHOPPING DISTRICT. AS FAST AS GATES TO STOREFRONTS ARE CLOSED SHUT, THEY ARE RIPPED FROM THEIR HINGES BY THE MOBS WHO ARE LOOKING TO STOCK UP ON PROVISIONS **AND** LUXURY ITEMS.

THE VERY NEXT DAY, NEW, ENTHUSIASTIC DJ CREWS BEGIN SPRINGING UP ON EVERY BLOCK IN THE BRONX... AND THEY **ALL** NOW HAVE EQUIPMENT COMPARABLE TO **DJ HOLLYWOOD.**

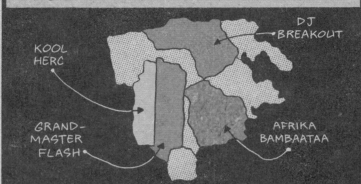

KOOL HERC, GRANDMASTER FLASH, AFRIKA BAMBAATAA, AND DJ BREAKOUT EACH HAVE CARVED A PIECE OF THE BRONX WHERE THEY SPECIALIZE. THE STYLE OF EACH OF THEIR PARTIES IS COMPLETELY DIFFERENT IN A MUSICAL SENSE.

DJ BREAKOUT

KOOL HERC

GRAND-MASTER FLASH

AFRIKA BAMBAATAA

HERC, BEING THE ORIGINATOR, IS THE ONE DJ THAT HAS PEOPLE FROM ALL NEIGHBORING TERRITORIES FLOCKING TO EXPERIENCE THE VIBE HE CREATES.

I GOTTA HEAD OUT FOR TEN MINUTES.

I'LL HOLD IT DOWN, COKE.

WELL KNOWN FOR HIS LEADERSHIP ABILITY AND INTIMIDATING STATURE, HERC'S EVENTS ARE LARGELY PEACEFUL, UNTIL THIS DAY.

BEEITCH!

!?

YOU IN THE WRONG PLACE WITH THAT KIND OF FOOLISHNESS!

ANGRY!

THE DAMAGE IS DONE IN SECONDS AND IT TAKES THE CULPRIT ABOUT AS LONG TO DEMATERIALIZE FROM THE SCENE.

BY THE TIME COKE LA ROCK GETS BACK TO THE VENUE, HERC IS ALREADY ON HIS WAY TO THE HOSPITAL.

IMMA KILL THE MUTHAFUCKA!

COKE MAKES IT TO THE HOSPITAL IN MINUTES. JUST BEFORE BEING WHEELED INTO SURGERY, KOOL HERC MAKES A PLEA TO HIS EMCEE.

Koff... Coke, I know who did it. Don't do... NOTHING.. KOFF... give my daddy ...YA GUN for TO...night.

OKAY...

KOOL HERC'S **ABSENCE** LEAVES A VOID THAT THE OTHER DJ'S QUICKLY FILL. **MOST** PEOPLE ARE SPECIFICALLY IN **AWE** OF GRANDMASTER FLASH'S **VIRTUOSITY** ON THE **WHEELS OF STEEL**, BUT HE IS **LACKING** IN ONE AREA...

HE'S SO PREOCCUPIED WITH CUTTING AND MIXING AND SCRATCHING RECORDS THAT HE DOESN'T EVEN KNOW WHAT TO SAY ON THE MICROPHONE.

THIS VACANCY DOESN'T GO UNNOTICED BY ENTERPRISING B-BOYS LOOKING TO HELP.

YEAH, GO FLASH! UH HUH...

GET THE FUCK OFF!

IT ISN'T UNTIL **COWBOY*** ENLISTS HIS SERVICES THAT RESULTS ARE FAVORABLE, THANKS TO HIS CHARISMA AND INNOVATION.

THROW YA HANDS IN THE **AIR**, AND WAVE 'EM LIKE YA JUST DON'T **CARE**!!

* GOT THE NICKNAME BECAUSE HE WALKS BOW-LEGGED.

2 B-BOY BROTHERS, **KID CREOLE** & **MELLE MEL**, LOVE THIS NEW ELEMENT TO FLASH'S SHOW. IT'S DOWNRIGHT INSPIRING TO KID CREOLE.

WE SHOULD BE UP THERE, TOO, MEL.

RELAX. WE DOIN' JUS' FINE HERE.

FLASH LIKES CREOLE FOR HIS ABILITY TO RHYME AND PATTER **NONSTOP.**

YES YES Y'ALL!

YA DON'T STOP!

MC'ING IS LIKE JAZZ IN ITS IMPROVISATION. MELLE MEL CAN SEE THE ATTRACTION OF BEING IN FRONT OF A CROWD, BUT HE'D LIKE A SAFETY NET...

... HE FINDS THAT WRITING RHYMES COMES **NATURAL** TO HIM, WHICH HELPS GIVE HIM THE **CONFIDENCE** TO GET ON STAGE WITH HIS BROTHER AND CREW. HIS TALENT ON THE MIC IS **COMPARABLE** TO **FLASH'S** SKILL ON THE TURNTABLES.

ITALIAN, CAUCASIAN, JAPAN**ESE**, SPANISH, INDIAN, NEGRO, AND VIETNAMESE. MC'S, DISK JOCKEYS...

...TO ALL THE FLY KIDS AND THE YOUNG LAY-**DEEZ**...

WHAT DICTATES THE QUALITY OF A PARTY, AT THIS STAGE, HAS NOTHING TO DO WITH THE EMCEE'S LYRICS. THE SPECIFICS OF THE RECORDS PLAYED MATTER LITTLE. THE DECIBEL LEVEL OF THE MUSIC IS PROBABLY MOST IMPORTANT. IF B-BOYS CAN'T HEAR YOU, THEN HOW ARE THEY SUPPOSED TO DANCE TO YOUR GROOVE?

DJ BREAKOUT IS A B-BOY WHO IS SLOWLY MAKING THE TRANSITION TO PLAYING RECORDS BY AMASSING A COLLECTION OF ALL THE MUSIC KOOL HERC USES.

THIS LOOKS LIKE IT, I GUESS. MAN, HERC'S A PUNK FOR TAKING THE LABELS OFF HIS RECORDS.

HIS SOUND SYSTEM IS MODEST, BUT HE'S FIGURED OUT "WORK-AROUNDS" FOR NOT HAVING BOUTIQUE ITEMS LIKE A MIXING BOARD.

IF YOU LOOK CLOSE ENOUGH TO A RECORD YOU CAN SEE WHERE THE "GET DOWN" PART IS, AND JUS' DROP THE NEEDLE ON IT.

BREAKOUT DOESN'T LET HIS TECHNICAL OR FINANCIAL HANDICAPS STOP HIS DJ'ING PURSUITS.

MY MILK CRATE SPEAKERS IS BUTTER!

AS HE ACCUMULATES HIS PLAYLIST OF BEATS, HIS PAL K.K. ROCKWELL HANGS OUT AND PRACTICES HIS RHYMES OVER THE MUSIC.

LIKE HOT BUTTAH ON... SAY WHAT, THE POPCORN.

K.K. PARLAYS HIS SHARPENED MICROPHONE SKILLS TO WORK WITH DJ BARON, WHO PLAYS SMALL PARTIES IN GYMS AND PARKS ACROSS THE BRONX.

...K.K. ROCKWELL, KNOWN TO RAISE A LOTTA HELL, AN' I LOVE TO MAKE LOVE TO THE JOLLY FEMALES.

STANDING ON A MILK CRATE

BREAKOUT COMES TO A FEW OF THE BARON/ROCKWELL PARTIES AND IS IMPRESSED. SOON, BOTH DJ'S CONSOLIDATE EQUIPMENT AND RECORDS TO FORM "THE BROTHERS DISCO" TO SOME SUCCESS. K.K. IS ALSO PART OF THE PACKAGE TO LEND SUPPORT ON THE MIC.

LIKE A LIME TO A LEMON

...A LEMON TO A LIME...

BROTHERS DISCO

JUST BECAUSE THE GROUP GAINS POPULARITY DOESN'T MEAN THEY BECOME MORE DISCIPLINED.

GET UP, BREAKOUT! THE REKKID'S ALMOST DONE!

PLAYING TO BIGGER CROWDS HELPS TO FINANCE MORE EQUIPMENT AND ALSO ATTRACTS FREE-LANCE TALENT LIKE **BUSY BEE STARSKI**, WHO OFFERS HIS ABILITY TO ANY DJ WITH A CERTAIN CRITICAL MASS.

WHERE'S THE PLACE WE WORK IT OUT?

AT THE ALPS!

AT THE ALPS!*

AT THE ALPS!

* THE ALPS IS A CHEAP HOTEL IN THE BRONX WHERE COUPLES RETREAT FOR SEXUAL CONGRESS.

THE CREW CAPTURES THE ATTENTION OF **AFRIKA BAMBAATAA**, WHO DECIDES TO ENGAGE THEM IN BATTLE. BEING RECOGNIZED BY THE **ZULU NATION** IS A FEATHER IN THE CAP FOR THE BROTHERS DISCO, **BUT** IT GOES WITHOUT SAYING THAT THEY WEREN'T PREPARED FOR THIS FIGHT.

BREAKOUT'S BROTHER, **JAZZY DEE**, WITNESSED THE SMACKDOWN AND IS ELECTED TO HELP MANAGE THE CREW.

GOTCH Y'ALL A PROPER MIXER.

YA OWE ME $500 FROM YA PROCEEDS...

THEIR FRIEND, AND FELLOW DJ, **TONY TONE**, IS AN EXCELLENT SOUND MAN, WHO HELPS BUILD UP THEIR SYSTEM WITH NEW EQUIPMENT AND FOUND OBJECTS.

WHAT IS YOU DOING WIT' DEM GAW-BITCH CANS?

YOU'LL SEE.

They call their system "**THE MIGHTY MIGHTY SASQUATCH**," and the Brothers Disco are **NOT** going to be made into fools ever again.

DJ DISCO WIZ and **CASANOVA FLY** realize that they need to make some changes to their organization if they want to remain competitive.

Yo, Wiz, man. We need to get us a manager, man.

Eavesdropping on the conversation is **HENRY JACKSON**, a bouncer from a local nightclub...

I'll be your manager, Caz.

Buy us a big ass sound system and we can talk.

IN GRANDMASTER FLASH'S NEIGHBORHOOD, A TEEN NAMED BILLY ENLISTED HIMSELF INTO THE MILITARY AND HE'S HEADING OFF TO BOOTCAMP AFTER THIS WEEKEND. FLASH, HIS 3 EMCEES, AND THE BRONX CELEBRATE THEIR FRIEND THE BEST WAY THEY CAN:

THIS IS FOR OUR MAIN MAN!

TO KEEP THE CROWD AWARE OF THE REASON THEY'RE ALL THERE, COWBOY CREATES A SPECIAL, SLIGHTLY SATIRICAL ROUTINE FOR THIS PARTY. COWBOY, MELLE MEL, AND KID CREOLE REPEAT THE ACT EVERY HALF HOUR FOR THE DURATION OF THE GET-TOGETHER.

LEFT... ...RIGHT... ...LEFT... ...RIGHT... ...HIP... ...HOP... ...DON'T... ...STOP...

BILLY!

AFTER THE SHOW, FOR WEEKS AND WEEKS, THE PEOPLE AT THE PARTY DEVELOPED SOME SHORTHAND WHEN RECALLING THE EXPERIENCE.

WAS YOU AT BILLY'S HIP HOP JAM?

I WAS THERE! HIP... HOP... HIP... HOP... DON'T... STOP! HA HA!

SOMEWHERE IN THE BRONX

YO, MONEY, I EVER TELL YOU HOW LOVEBUG STARSKI MADE UP THE WORD "HIP HOP"?

RUSSELL "RUSH" SIMMONS, BEING THE ONLY MAN TO PROMOTE SHOWS IN QUEENS, ENJOYS HIS STRONGHOLD. HE DOES HIT SNAGS FROM TIME TO TIME, HOWEVER...

RUN! HOW COULD YOU DO THITH?

YOU GOT A SHOW WIT' KURTITH THITH WEEKEN'!!!

IT WAS A ACCIDENT, RUSSELL.

ME AND D KNOW SOMEBODY ILL ON THE WHEELS. HE GOT 12 CRATES OF REKKIDS, TOO.

12 CRATE'TH OF REKKIDTH?! BAMBAATAA ONLY HATH 20 HITH THELF!

FLASH ONLY HAS SEVENTEEN CRATES. WHO IS THIS CAT?

DAVY DMX. HE PLAYS IN THE PARK.

DARRYL McDANIELS

THE ONLY TIME DAVY DMX DOESN'T PLAY MUSIC TO THE PEOPLE IN THE PARK IS WHEN HE'S PLAYING GUITAR IN CHURCH.

HIS EMCEES, COOL-T AND HURRICANE, "SOLO SOUNDS," COMPLEMENT THE MUSIC WELL...

ROCKS THIS PLACE.

HURRICANE'S GOT CLOUT!

KURTIS BLOW IS THE BIGGEST STAR IN HOLLIS, QUEENS, THOUGH, SO IT'S NO SURPRISE THAT DAVY DMX ACCEPTS THE OFFER TO BE HIS DJ.

HE'S A DISCO DREAM ON THE MEAN MACHINE!

A HANDFUL OF DJ'S BEGIN TO FILL THE HOLE DMX LEFT IN THE PARKS AND PLAYGROUNDS. NOW YOUNG JASON MIZELL CAN MASTER HIS CRAFT PUBLICLY.

"JAM MASTER".

...CUT FASTER!

16

WHERE DOO-WOP SINGERS HAD ONCE STOOD, RAPPERS NOW ADORN THE STREET CORNERS OF HARLEM.

...GET SICK, FROM THE FLIP OF MY LIP...

BEING THE OWNER OF HIS OWN RECORD LABEL, **PAUL WINLEY** IS WELL AWARE OF THIS PARADIGM SHIFT.

IF SO MANY PEOPLE WEREN'T DOING IT FOR FREE, I'D THINK ABOUT MAKING A RECORD.

RAPPING EVEN SURROUNDS HIM AT HOME.

TANYA-BABY. YOU STILL DOING YOUR HOMEWORK?

I'M WRITING RHYMES, DADDY.

HIS BUSINESS IS ALSO AFFECTED BY THIS DYNAMIC, NEW CULTURE.

WE SOLD OUT OF **WHAT?** THOSE RECORDS HAVE BEEN COLLECTING DUST FOR YEARS.

THE SHOPS ARE BECOMING HIP TO THE NEEDS OF THE DJ.

I STARTED THIS REFERENCE BINDER OF BREAKS FOR THE KIDS.

...YOU MEAN TO TELL ME YOU'RE ABLE TO MARK THESE RECORDS UP $20, $30 AND NOT ONLY DO THEY SELL, **BUT** THESE DJ'S WILL BUY TWO COPIES?!

WILL YOU TELL ME WHAT THE MOST IMPORTANT "BREAKS" ARE?

IN SHORT ORDER, WINLEY COMPILES THESE COVETED SONGS INTO A SINGLE RECORD.

THE TRACK LISTING:

BOB JAMES: TAKE ME TO THE MARDI GRAS

PAT LUNDY: WORK SONG

THE J.B'S: BLOW YOUR HEAD

THE MAGIC DISCO MACHINE: SCRATCHIN'

NEW BIRTH: GOT TO GET A KNUTT

NEW BIRTH: I CAN UNDERSTAND IT

CREATIVE SOURCE: CORAZON

DENNIS COFFEY AND THE DETROIT GUITAR BAND: SCORPIO

BECAUSE OF THE DUBIOUS LEGALITY OF THIS BOOTLEG GEM, WINLEY DISTRIBUTES **SUPER DISCO BRAKES** TO STORES IN A "LOW-KEY" MANNER AND URGES THEM TO KEEP THE RECORD BEHIND THE COUNTER. IN SPITE OF ALL THE CLOAK & DAGGER...

SORRY, BUB...

...**SOLD OUT!**

THIS SUCCESS FORCES PAUL TO RECONSIDER THINGS.

TANYA-BABY, WHY DON'T YA LET ME HEAR THOSE RHYMES OF YOURS.

K!

PRECIPITATION WOULD OBVIOUSLY BE A PROBLEM, BUT THE SIMPLE FRIGIDITY OF A NEW YORK NOVEMBER ISN'T ENOUGH TO KEEP **FLASH** AND HIS 3 MC'S FROM PLAYING FOR THEIR CROWD.

RAY CHANDLER HAPPENS TO WANDER NEAR, AT FIRST THINKING THAT THE PARTY IS A GANG FIGHT OR SOMETHING.

WHY Y'ALL PLAYIN' IN THE COLD LIKE THIS?

WHERE ELSE ARE WE GONNA PLAY?

CHANDLER RECENTLY OPENED A CLUB AND, WITH SOME COAXING, COMMISSIONS GRANDMASTER FLASH TO PLAY THE VENUE EACH WEEK.

PRETTY SOON **KOOL DJ AJ** SIGNS ON AS AN OPENING ACT. THE BUZZ ON THE STREET ABOUT **THE BLACK DOOR** CLUB PROMPTS **BUSY BEE STARSKI** TO JOIN AJ.

BUSY BEE MUST PERFORM EARLY BECAUSE HIS MOM HAS HIM ON A CURFEW.

MORE AND MORE PEOPLE FILL THE ROOM EACH WEEK AS FLASH WHIPS THEM INTO A BOMBASTIC FRENZY.

HUH? MY SPEAKER?

POP

COWBOY!

tHink i... NEED A D-doc...Tor... FLaSH...

IT TAKES WEEKS FOR **COWBOY** TO GET BACK ON STAGE. IN THE MEANTIME, A GROUP OF FORMER **BLACK SPADES** NOW KNOWN AS THE **CASANOVAS** BEGIN SHOWING UP AND THEY'RE NOT LOOKING TO PAY TO GAIN ENTRY TO CHANDLER'S BLACK DOOR VENUE.

I'LL DO Y'ALL ONE BETTER. KEEP THE CROWD PEACEFUL AND I'LL PAY YOU TO BE HERE.

YOU A SMART MUH-FUGGA, CHANDLER.

BRINGING GRANDMASTER FLASH AND HIS 3 MC'S INDOORS **AND** CHARGING PATRONS FOR THE PRIVILEGE TURNS OUT TO BE A LUCRATIVE GAME CHANGER.

VERY RAPIDLY THEY OUTGROW **THE BLACK DOOR** CLUB TO PLAY VENUES THREE TIMES THE SIZE TO ACCOMMODATE THEIR DEMAND.

Y'ALL DON'T THINK IT'S FUCKED UP THAT FLASH KEEPS SO MUCH LOOT FOR HISSELF?

HMMM?

THIS NEW POTENTIAL SOURCE OF INCOME, PLAYING THE NIGHTCLUB CIRCUIT, BECOMES MORE THAN JUST A CONSIDERATION FOR **THE BROTHERS DISCO** IN THE NORTH BRONX.

WE'LL FOLLOW THE FORMULA FLASH AND HIS MC'S PUT DOWN...

...BUT, WE'LL HAVE MORE DJ'S, MORE MC'S, AND A BIGGER SOUND SYSTEM!

AFTER A FEW AUDITIONS, DJ BARON AND DJ BREAKOUT WEAVE IN A NEW MC, **KEITH KEITH**, TO JOIN K.K. ROCKWELL AND THE MERCURIAL BUSY BEE ON THE MICROPHONE.

...BUT, YOU CAN CALL ME KEITH **CAESAR**, THE REASON WHY? CAUSE I'M THE WOMEN **PLEASER**!

STRATEGICALLY SETTING THEMSELVES APART FROM THE REST, THE BROTHERS DISCO INDUCT A FEMALE MC, **SHA-ROCK**, INTO THE GROUP. SHE COMES COMPLETE WITH HER OWN SECURITY FORCE.

WITH PRACTICE AND IMAGINATION, THE CREW CREATES A DECENT ACT FULL OF ROUTINES AND ANTICS. NIGHTCLUBS BEGIN TO WELCOME THEM WITH OPEN ARMS.

THE ONE PROBLEM WITH PLAYING LATE IS THAT BUSY BEE'S MOM **ROUTINELY** DRAGS HIM OUT OF THE VENUE FOR BREAKING CURFEW.

I'M GONNA MOVE ON, Y'ALL. THEODORE AND THE **L BROTHERS** NEED A FRESH EMCEE.

THE EXISTING MC'S SEEM TO JIVE MOST WITH DJ BREAKOUT. A FRUSTRATED DJ BARON MAKES SURE TO FIND AN MC WHO COMPLEMENTS **HIS** STYLE OF PLAY. **RAHIEM** FILLS THAT ROLE, TAKING BUSY BEE'S PLACE.

I'M HIP, THE DIP, THE WOMEN'S PIMP...

MY MAN!

ONCE THE TEAM GELS THEY TAKE **THE MIGHTY MIGHTY SASQUATCH** (THEIR SOUND SYSTEM) AROUND TOWN, BOOKING SHOWS AS **THE BROTHERS DISCO AND THE FUNKY FOUR MC'S.**

THEIR UNIQUE PRESENTATION EARNS THEM MONEY AND **NOTORIETY** AROUND THE BRONX AND QUEENS.

WE GONNA HAVE TO **CRUSH** THESE MUTHA FUCKAHS!

THIS **RAHIEM** CAT IS BUTTER.

WITH CLUBS IN NEIGHBORING BOROUGHS BOOKING DJ'S, MANHATTAN'S **DJ HOLLYWOOD** FEELS HIS CAT-BIRD SEAT MAY BE IN JEOPARDY. HE BEGINS PLAYING SOMETIMES 5 VENUES A NIGHT, MAKING AS MUCH AS $2000 IN AN EVENING.

HOLLY...

...WOOD! ..WOOD! ...WOOD! OD! ...WOOD! OD! WOOD! ...WOOD! ...WOOD! OD! ...WOOD! WOOD

HOLLYWOOD ISN'T WITHOUT SOME ADVERSITY, THOUGH. HIS MC, EDDIE CHEBA, AND HIS DJ PROTEGES, **JUNEBUG** AND **LOVEBUG STAR-SKI**, GET HIRED AWAY TO WORK A NIGHTCLUB IN THE BRONX CALLED **DISCO FEVER** IN AN EFFORT TO ATTRACT AN ADULT AUDIENCE.

SON, WHAT ARE YOU GONNA DO? EVERYONE LOOKS LIKE HOBOS WHO COME IN HERE!

I'M GONNA START CHARGING LESS OF A COVER FOR KIDS WHO COME IN DRESSED NICER.

EVERY MAJOR CREW EVENTUALLY PLAYS A CLUB CALLED "**THE SPARKLE**," WHERE HENRY "**BIG BANK HANK**" JACKSON WORKS AS A BOUNCER. A HUGE FAN, HE RECORDS TAPES OF HIS FAVORITE ROUTINES.

I'M IMP, THE DIMP. THE WOMEN'S PIMP!

THE WOMEN FIGHT FOR MY DELIGHT.

FOR GENERATIONS, YOUNG FRED'S FAMILY HAS MAINTAINED A PLACE OF HISTORIC SIGNIFICANCE. HIS GRANDFATHER WAS GOOD FRIENDS WITH **MARCUS GARVEY**, WHO INDUCTED HIM TO RUN THE BROOKLYN BRANCH OF THE UNIVERSAL NEGRO IMPROVEMENT ASSOCIATION.

FRED'S FATHER WAS IN THE **AUDUBON BALLROOM** WHEN MALCOLM X WAS ASSASSINATED. HE HEARD HIS FATHER'S WAR STORIES WHEN THE FAMILY WOULD ENTERTAIN JAZZ LEGENDS LIKE DIZZY GILLESPIE AND MILES DAVIS AT THEIR BEDFORD-STUYVESANT HOME.

ONE WONDERS WHAT **FRED BRATHWAITE'S** GODFATHER, BEBOP PIONEER **MAX ROACH**, THINKS OF THE YOUNG MAN'S CURRENT OBSESSION.

HE ROUTINELY SKIPS SCHOOL TO VISIT MUSEUMS AND ART GALLERIES (TAGGING "**BULL 99**" ALONG THE WAY). ON THIS DAY, DURING A POP ART EXHIBIT, FRED DISCOVERS AN IMPORTANT CORRELATION.

MAN, THE STUFF THIS **LICHTENSTEIN** DUDE DID...

...AIN'T NO DIFFERENT THAN WHEN A CAT PAINTS A FLY **VAUGHN BODE** CHARACTER ON THEIR BURNER.

NOBODY ELSE IS MAKING THIS CONNECTION! PEOPLE **HATE** THIS SHIT... MATTER OF FACT...

AS HE CONTINUES TO STUDY, IN THIS ARTISTIC CONTEXT, THERE IS ONE NAME THAT STANDS OUT FROM THE REST.

CURIOUS ABOUT THE IDENTITY OF THIS MYSTERIOUS ARTIST, THE WORD ON THE STREET LEADS FRED TO THIS LOWER EAST SIDE HIGH SCHOOL.

'SCUSE ME. I'M LOOKIN' FOR **LEE QUINONES**.

?

ARE YOU A COP? I WANT A LAWYER. I AIN'T SAYIN' NOTHIN'!

HA HA. NAW.

LEE, MAN, I KNOW WHO YOU ARE AND I'M DOWN WITH WHAT YOU DO. YOU AIN'T NO DIFFERENT THAN **PICASSO** IN MY BOOK.

ARE YOU A FUCKING COP, MAN?

LET'S GO PAINT.

ONCE LEE IS CONVINCED THAT FRED IS LEGIT, HE FOLDS BRATHWAITE INTO HIS ILLUSTRIOUS GRAFFITI CREW, **THE FABULOUS FIVE.** IN HONOR OF THIS NEW ASSOCIATION, BULL99 DROPS THIS MONIKER FOR A NEW ALIAS: **FRED FAB FIVE.** WITH THIS UNDERGROUND CREDIBILITY HE SHARES HIS THOUGHTS WITH NEW YORK CITY.

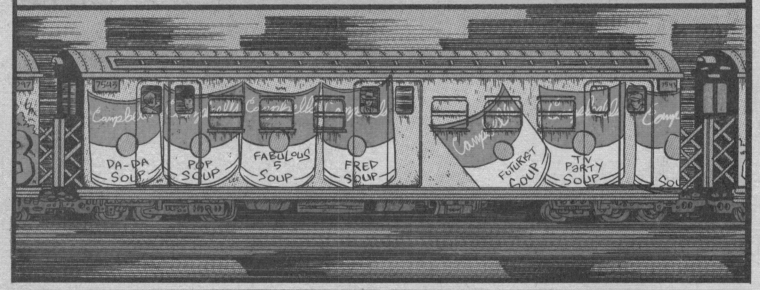

THE MEANING OF FRED'S **CAMPBELL'S SOUP TRAIN** ISN'T LOST ON **HENRY CHALFANT** AND **MARTHA COOPER**, WHO HAVE BEEN DOCUMENTING THIS VIBRANT, NEO-ART MOVEMENT TOGETHER, WITH LITTLE OR NO MAINSTREAM SUPPORT.

AS HIS TRAIN ROLLS ALONG, FRED GETS A PHONE CALL.

THE **VILLAGE VOICE** WANTS TO DO AN ARTICLE ON THIS GRAFF SHIT!

THINK IT'S THE **PIGS**? IT COULD BE A TRAP!

AT THIS JUNCTURE, THE CLUB SCENE IS THOUGHT OF AS THE **MAJOR LEAGUES** FOR HIP HOP PERFORMERS IN THE BRONX.

THE PARKS AND GYMS ARE STILL VIBRANT LOCALES FOR GOOD PARTIES. ONE OF THE BEST CREWS AT THE OUTDOOR JAMS IS THE **L BROTHERS**, MADE UP OF FLASH'S PROTEGE, THEODORE, HIS OLD PAL MEAN GENE, AND THEIR BROTHER, CORDIE-O.

WORD TRAVELS ABOUT YOUNG THEODORE'S PRODIGIOUS TALENT ON THE WHEELS OF STEEL. LACKING MC'S AT THEIR SHOWS, KEVVY KEV AND MASTER ROB, ANOTHER SET OF BLOOD BROTHERS, FILL THAT POSITION. AS THEY GAIN POPULARITY, BUSY BEE STARSKI JOINS THEM ON THE MIC.

THE L BROTHERS BECOME WELL KNOWN ENOUGH TO APPEAR ON GRANDMASTER FLASH'S RADAR. HE DECIDES HE'S HAD ENOUGH OF THEM AND CALLS THE NEW GROUP OUT TO BATTLE, DRAGGING AS MUCH EQUIPMENT AS POSSIBLE FROM THE CLUB TO THE DUEL.

FLASH BE CHEATIN'!

THE SHOWDOWN TAKES PLACE IN NEUTRAL **ZULU NATION** TERRITORY. ANGERED BY FLASH'S BREACH OF ETIQUETTE, AFRIKA BAMBAATAA HELPS THE L BROTHERS EVEN THE SCALE, AS THE CROWD IS ALREADY ACCLIMATED TO HIS PLAYLIST.

PLAY THIS REKKID. RIGHT HERE AT THIS SPOT. TRUST ME.

THE PINK PANTHER THEME SONG?

AFTER THE L BROTHERS EMERGE AS THE VICTORS, THEIR NOTORIETY EARNS THEM A CHANCE INSIDE THE CLUB GAME.

WHERE THE FUCKIN' DJ AT?

A SHOOTOUT OCCURS AT ONE OF THEIR SHOWS, RESULTING IN THE DEATH OF A POWERFUL DRUG DEALER'S SIBLING. THEODORE AND CREW DECIDE TO STAY OUT OF THE SPOTLIGHT FOR AN INDEFINITE LENGTH OF TIME.

GRANDMASTER FLASH AND HIS 3 MC'S NEXT TARGET IN THEIR QUEST FOR DOMINATION IS THE BROTHERS DISCO AND THE FUNKY FOUR MC'S. EACH CREW IS TALENTED. EACH CREW HAS LOYAL FOLLOWINGS. AND BOTH GROUPS HAVE ENOUGH MUSCLE AND SECURITY THAT THEY DON'T HAVE TO WORRY ABOUT ANY "STICK-UP KIDS" THREATENING THEIR POSITIONS.

GRANDMASTER FLASH

MELLE MEL

COWBOY

KID CREOLE

FUNKY FOUR

K.K. ROCKWELL

KEITH KEITH

SHA-ROCK

RAHIEM

BROTHERS DISCO

DJ BARON

DJ BREAKOUT

THE MAJOR FACTORS THAT PUT FLASH AND HIS GUYS OVER THE TOP ARE THEIR PSYCHOLOGY AND ACCUMULATED EXPERIENCE.

THE BEATDOWN IS MERCILESS AND HARD TO WATCH, AS THE FUNKY FOUR GET THEIR HEARTS TAKEN.

THROUGH THE ONSLAUGHT, FLASH AND MELLE MEL ARE EXTREMELY IMPRESSED WITH RAHIEM'S BRAVADO, SO THEY APPROACH HIM TO JOIN THE CREW. LET DOWN BY THE FUNKY FOUR'S WEAK PERFORMANCE, RAHIEM'S CHOICE IS EASY. NOT LONG AFTER, MR. NESS/SCORPIO FOLLOWS RAHIEM AND THEY ESTABLISH THEMSELVES AS GRANDMASTER FLASH AND THE FURIOUS FIVE.

RAHIEM ISN'T THE ONLY CASUALTY IN THE BROTHERS DISCO'S ORGANIZATION.

I JUST AIN'T FEELIN' IT, NOW...

K.K. ROCKWELL RAPIDLY RECRUITS A FEW HIGH-SCHOOL FRIENDS, JAZZY JEFF AND RODNEY C, INTO THE GROUP, SO THAT THEY CAN MAINTAIN A PRESENCE IN THE CLUBS.

AIN'T NUTHIN' TO IT BUT TO DO IT!

SHA-ROCK CAN'T HELP BUT REJOIN AFTER SEEING THE DYNAMISM OF THESE NEW ADDITIONS. THEY OVERCOME NOMENCLATURAL SNAGS AND PROTECT THEIR "BRAND" BY CALLING THEMSELVES FUNKY FOUR PLUS ONE.

KEITH KEITH

24

NOBODY CAN ACCUSE **BOBBY ROBINSON** OF BEING ANYTHING LESS THAN A BRILLIANT AND ENTREPRENEURIAL MAN. AFTER THE WAR, HE BECAME THE FIRST BLACK MAN TO OPEN A BUSINESS, THIS RECORD SHOP, IN **HARLEM**... ON 125TH ST., NOT FAR FROM THE **APOLLO THEATER**, TO BE EXACT. HE'S ALSO A RECORD PRODUCER, CREATING LABELS FOR MUSICIANS BASED ON GENRES THAT SELL WELL AT THE STORE.

THE STRATEGIC LOCATION OF BOBBY'S SHOP ALLOWS FOR A WIDE-RANGING CLIENTELE, WHICH INCLUDES THE OCCASIONAL CELEBRITY.

THANKS FOR SIGNING IT FOR THE BOY, HOLLYWOOD.

TELL SPOONIE TO KEEP THEM GRADES UP!

Ba-Bo

ROBINSON HAS RAISED HIS NEPHEW, GABRIEL JACKSON, FOR YEARS. THE BOY AND HIS FRIENDS HAVE A SPECIFIC APPRECIATION FOR **HIP HOP**, BASED ON THE DJ HOLLYWOOD AND LOVEBUG STARSKI MIX TAPES THAT FLOAT THROUGH HIS UNCLE'S HANDS.

MY NAME IS MC **SPOONIE GEE** AS YOU CAN **SEE**...

GABRIEL'S NICKNAME IS "**SPOONIE**" BECAUSE HE DOESN'T USE ANY OTHER UTENSILS WHILE EATING.

NO, RAPPIN' AT THE DINNER TABLE, NOW!

A SMALL-TIME RECORD PRODUCER, PETER BROWN, STOPS BY THE STORE TO SPITBALL DIFFERENT IDEAS TO BOBBY.

YOU WANT TO RECORD THAT RAP SHIT? **HA!**

ANYBODY CAN RAP FOR **FREE!** SPOONIE RAPS ALL DAY AND NIGHT.

SEE WHAT I MEAN, PETER? IT'S **KID** STUFF. AND KIDS DON'T HAVE MONEY TO BUY **NOTHING.**

SPOONIE GEE AND HIS FRIENDS **KOOL MOE DEE** AND **L.A. SUNSHINE** SHARE THE REPUTATION OF BEING THE BEST RAPPERS IN NORMAN THOMAS HIGH SCHOOL. BETTER KNOWN AS THE **TREACHEROUS THREE**, THE GROUP HAS LITTLE COMPETITION.

SPECIAL K! YOU HARD AS HELL!

HE ALMOST AS GOOD AS YOU, **MOE**.

MAN! I'LL SERVE THAT CHUMP!

HA HA

THE NEXT DAY DURING LUNCH, **SPECIAL K** FINDS OUT ABOUT MOE DEE'S SPITFIRE LYRICAL ABILITY.

A RAPPIN' **LORD**, I'M NOT A **BORE**. THE BADDEST MAN YOU EVER **SAW!**

THE MONEY **MAKIN'**, EARTH QUAKIN', MAN WHO GETS THE PARTY SHAKIN'!

THOUGH HE LOST THE BATTLE, SPECIAL K CAN'T HELP BUT BE INSPIRED BY HIS OPPONENT'S TALENT. HE RUNS HOME TO TRY AND CREATE HIS OWN MACHINE-GUN RAP STYLE. K'S BROTHER, **T LA ROCK**, HAS BEEN SNOOPING ON HIM FOR HOURS.

HARD ROCK JUNKY AND RHYTHM FANATIC

SHIT'S DEF!!

B-BOY ACROBATIC

SPECIAL K CANNOT **WAIT** TO CORNER MOE DEE!

!

EQUAL SHARIN' ALWAYS CARIN' MAN WHO RHYMES WITH ALL THE DARIN'... SATISFACTION GUARANTEED! GIVIN' YOU JUS' WHAT YOU NEED. I'M SPECIAL K WITH ALL THE...

EACH EARNING THE OTHER MAN'S RESPECT, THE TWO EMCEES BECOME INSEPARABLE.

ONCE ME AND THE TREACHEROUS START PLAYING SHOWS I WANT YOU TO WARM UP THE CROWD!

BUTTER!

BY DAY, 23-YEAR-OLD JOHN RIVAS WORKS LONG HOURS CUSTOM BUILDING SPEAKERS AT AN ELECTRONICS STORE IN THE MIDDLE OF MANHATTAN.

THESE SPEAKERS WILL ROCK THE HOUSE. THANKS JOHNNY!

HIS INTIMATE KNOWLEDGE OF SOUND EQUIPMENT WORKS TO HIS BENEFIT AS HE MOONLIGHTS, SPINNING RECORDS UNDER THE NAME LUCKY THE MAGICIAN.

SAY HO!

INTERESTED IN HONING HIS SKILLS ON THE MICROPHONE, "LUCKY" ENROLLS IN CLASSES AT THE NEW YORK SCHOOL OF ANNOUNCING AND SPEECH.

NETWORKING WITH PEERS AT SCHOOL, HE LEARNS...

YEAH, LUCKY, WHBI BROADCASTS FROM THE UPPER WEST SIDE. THEY SELL AIRTIME TOO. $75 AN HOUR.

IT DOESN'T TAKE LONG FOR JOHN TO FIND SPONSORS. HIS MANAGER AT THE STORE KNOWS THAT HE ALREADY COMMANDS A DECENT CROWD AT HIS PARTIES.

WHAT WILL $100 GET ME, SON?

FOUR COMMERCIAL SPOTS.

HEY, PUT ME DOWN FOR A HANDFUL OF SPOTS. I RUN THE SEAFOOD JOINT ACROSS THE WAY...

STARTING OFF ALREADY MAKING MONEY, LUCKY THE MAGICIAN STREAMLINES HIS HANDLE TO MR. MAGIC. ON SUNDAY NIGHTS FROM 2AM - 4AM HE HOSTS...

DISCO SHOWCASE, Y'ALL!

AS MR. MAGIC FINDS HIS NICHE, HE STARTS INVITING HIP HOP PERFORMERS TO VISIT THE PROGRAM.

FLASH CUTS THE RECORD DOWN TO THE BONE...

MAGIC'S SHOW BECOMES AN IMPORTANT VENUE TO GET THE WORD OUT.

IF YOU LIKED WHAT YOU HEARD, KURTITH ITH PLAYING THE HOTEL DIPLOMAT NECKTHT WEEKEND.

27

ON ONE CONDITION, **BIG BANK HANK** HAS THE OPPORTUNITY TO BECOME CASANOVA FLY'S MANAGER. HANK MUST RESORT TO HIS LAST OPTION IN HIS QUEST TO GET CAZ A BIGGER, BETTER SOUND SYSTEM.

...MORNIN' DAD?

HIS DAD GIVES IN AND NOW **CAZ** AND **THE MIGHTY FORCE** CAN FINALLY COMPARE TO THE LIKES OF FLASH, BAMBAATAA, AND BREAKOUT.

CASANOVA FLY BECOMES A **GRANDMASTER** IN HIS OWN RIGHT, BY BEING ABLE TO SPIT OUT CLEVER RHYMES **AND** KEEP THE BEAT AT THE SAME TIME.

...MASTER OF THE CEREMONY! NOT A FAKE AND NOT A PHONY!

IT'S A HECK OF A SIGHT TO WITNESS, BUT THE PRESSURE HANK FEELS TO PAY BACK HIS DAD IS STRONGER THAN THE AURA THAT CAZ CREATES PUBLICLY.

THOSE ARE ALL JUST DOLLAR BILLS?

WHATCHOO THINK, HANK? Y'ALL ONLY BE CHARGING $2 A HEAD.

HIP HOP MANAGEMENT ISN'T QUITE PAYING THE DIVIDENDS THAT HE EXPECTED, SO HANK GETS A DAY JOB.

GET A MOVE ON, HENRY!

♪♫!♩ ♩♫?

COMING RIGHT UP!

THE MUSIC IS STILL OMNIPRESENT, THOUGH, THANKS TO THE TAPES CAZ RECORDED FOR HANK TO USE FOR PRESS KITS.

I GOT A LINCOLN CONTINENTAL... AL D A SUNROOF CADILLAC!

Call the fever

ROCKY FORD IS ONE OF THE ONLY PEOPLE AT **BILLBOARD MAGAZINE** EQUIPPED TO HANDLE A STORY IDEA REVOLVING AROUND THE NEW "BREAK BEAT" FAD. HE DOESN'T KNOW MUCH ABOUT IT, **BUT** HE'S INTERESTED.

RUSH PRODUCTIONS SEEMS TO BE BEHIND EVERY MAJOR SHOW...

ON ONE FRUITFUL DAY, ROCKY CATCHES UP WITH THE KID RESPONSIBLE FOR WALLPAPERING **QUEENS** WITH ALL THOSE PROMOTIONAL FLYERS. TURNS OUT IT'S YOUNG, RETIRED **DJ RUN**.

HAVE YOUR BIG BROTHER GIVE ME A CALL...

FORD BECOMES FAST FRIENDS WITH **RUSSELL "RUSH" SIMMONS**. BOTH BEING INTELLIGENT GUYS, THEY SEE THAT THEIR UNION IS MUTUALLY BENEFICIAL.

RUSSELL, I CAN'T BELIEVE HOW MANY PEOPLE YOU GET TO COME TO YOUR PARTIES, MAN!

IT'TH NUT'TH, I KNOW.

CLEARLY WITNESSING SOMETHING **BIG** BUBBLING TO THE SURFACE, ROCKY SACRIFICES HIS GIG AT THE MAGAZINE. HIS **INSPIRATION** IS PALPABLE.

I WANT TO PRODUCE A RECORD WITH DJ HOLLYWOOD AND EDDIE CHEBA.

THEM GUY'TH AWE THUCKA'TH! YOU SHOULD RECORD MY MAN, KURTITH BLOW.

DJ HOLLYWOOD'S POPULARITY HAS BEEN ON A STEADY INCLINE FOR A WHILE, THANKS TO PLAYING 5 TIMES A NIGHT AT VENUES ALL AROUND TOWN.

HIS **SWAGGER** AND **EGO** DON'T EVEN FALTER WHEN HE HAS THE CHANCE TO WARM UP FOR BIG, NATIONAL ACTS.

GIVE ME SOME OF THAT YUMMY YUM YUM...

...BEFORE I GO TO BED!

BILL CURTIS AND HIS FATBACK BAND ARE IN ATTENDANCE THIS PARTICULAR NIGHT. THEY'RE AMAZED BY HOW THE CROWD CONTINUOUSLY SCREAMS FOR HOLLYWOOD AS THE HEADLINERS TRY TO GET THROUGH THEIR SET.

HOLLY...

..WOOD!

CURTIS BEGINS SEEING HIP HOP MORE AND MORE ON AN EVERYDAY BASIS.

♫ ♪♪♪
♫♫♫!

... LIKE A BOLT OF LIGHTNING AND A STREAK OF HEAT... I'LL ROCK...

HMMM...

IN THE STUDIO, THE FATBACK BAND HAS HIT A NEAR IMPENETRABLE ROADBLOCK WHILE WORKING ON THEIR SONG "CATCH THE BEAT."

WHAT IF WE PUT SOME KIND OF GUY RAPPING OVER THE TRACK?

WILD!

MY MAN TIM IS ONE BAD MUTHA!

BRING 'IM ON BY.

DJ HOLLYWOOD'S APPRENTICE, LOVEBUG STARSKI, IS PLAYING A VENUE CALLED HARLEM WORLD, WHICH HAS JUST UNDER-GONE A MAKEOVER, TRANSITIONING FROM DISCO TO HIP HOP.

HIP DA HOP DA HIPPY HIPPY HOP DA HOP HOP HIP...

...MORE PEOPLE HERE THAN USUAL...

THE OCCASION IS A BIRTHDAY PARTY FOR FORMER CHILD SINGER/ CURRENT SONG WRITER AND RECORD PRODUCER SYLVIA ROBINSON. THIS IS HER INTRODUCTION TO HIP HOP AND SHE IMMEDIATELY RECOGNIZES THE VALUE IN IT.

THANK YOU, LORD!

IT'S NOT TYPICAL FOR **PAUL WINLEY** TO SPEND EXTRA TIME AND MONEY IN THE RECORDING STUDIO, BUT TODAY HE'S DECIDED TO HAVE HIS HOUSE BAND, THE **HARLEM UNDERGROUND BAND**, CREATE AN INSTRUMENTAL TRACK FOR HIM AFTER A LONG DAY AT WORK.

WHAT FOR, BOSS?

I HAVE A **PROJECT** IN MIND FOR MY **DAUGHTERS**.

BET?

BEING AT AN EPISCOPAL SUMMER CAMP DOESN'T STOP YOUNG **CURT "FLIRT"** AND **ED "LOVER"** FROM PULLING THEIR USUAL CAPERS.

MAN, HE'S **PUNKIN' OUT** ON US!

CHILL OUT, CURT. HE HAS THE STUFF ALREADY. HE'S JUST BUSY.

HE A BIG **LIAR**. I BET HIS DAD DON'T EVEN MAKE MOVIES.

YOU'RE RIGHT. HIS **UNCLE** MAKES 'EM.

CAMP DeWolfe

HEY GUYS!

TED DEMME, THE ONLY WHITE BOY THEY'RE FRIENDS WITH WHO KNOWS **HIP HOP**, IS HAPPY TO INDULGE IN CONSPIRACY. THIS NIGHT, HOWEVER, HAS A MORE SOMBER TONE.

WE'RE GONNA **NEED** THIS! I JUST GOT OFF THE PHONE...

...MY FRIEND BACK HOME TOLD ME GRANDMASTER FLASH AND THE FURIOUS FIVE **BROKE UP**!

FUCK! I WANTED TO SEE THEM PLAY AT **THE FEVER** WHEN I'M OLD ENOUGH!

THERE'S STILL A COUPLE OF **BOOTLEGS** WE DON'T HAVE YET, AT LEAST!

glug...

FLASH AND HIS CREW HAD A CRITICAL MASS, TOO. IT'S JUST THAT THE FURIOUS ISN'T HAPPY WITH THEIR FINANCIAL CUT.

$75 A SHOW IS BULLSHIT.

FUCK CHANDLER...

FUCK FLASH!

...AND THE CASANOVAS!

IT TAKES NO TIME AT ALL FOR **MELLE MEL** AND THE **FURIOUS FIVE** TO FIND NEW, EXCITED DJ'S TO WORK WITH. **TONY TONE** FROM THE **BROTHERS DISCO** RECENTLY HOOKED UP WITH LATINO DJ **CHARLIE CHASE** TO PUT TOGETHER A SET. ALL 7 HIP HOPPERS SEEM TO MESH WELL.

FLASH'S PARTNER AND PROMOTER **RAY CHANDLER** ISN'T HAPPY WITH THE SPLIT. HE SENDS HIS SECURITY FORCE, **THE CASANOVAS**, TO TALK SOME SENSE INTO THE DEFECTORS.

!

NEEDLESS TO SAY, FLASH AND THE FURIOUS FIVE **AREN'T** APART FOR VERY LONG.

HOW MUCH YOU THINK YOU WORTH, FOO?

$75

SYLVIA ROBINSON, STILL INCREDIBLY INSPIRED BY WHAT SHE SAW AT **HARLEM WORLD**, BEGINS PUTTING OUT FEELERS TO THE HIP HOP PERFORMERS THAT SHE IS FAMILIAR WITH.

LOVEBUG STARSKI

A RECORD? YOU CAN'T PAY ME MORE THAN I MAKE AT MY SHOWS, CAN YOU?

GRANDMASTER FLASH

WHO WOULD WANT TO BUY A RECORD OF ONE OF OUR PARTIES?

WE AIN'T INTERESTED.

FRED FAB FIVE'S VILLAGE VOICE ARTICLE YIELDS SOME GREAT CONNECTIONS, LIKE THE ITALIAN ART DEALER WHO BRINGS HIM TO **ROME** AND SELLS HIS PAINTINGS OUT AT $1000 A POP.

WHEN HE GETS BACK TO **NEW YORK**, FRED BECOMES A REGULAR FACE IN THE MANHATTAN **ART WORLD**.

JEAN-MICHEL WRITES GRAFF, TOO.

MICHAEL HOLMAN

WORD! WHATCHOO WRITE?

SAMO...

FRED AND **BASQUIAT** ALSO RUN AROUND TOWN WITH **GLENN O'BRIEN**, EDITOR OF **ANDY WARHOL'S** INTERVIEW MAGAZINE. GLENN IS ALSO THE GUY RESPONSIBLE FOR STEERING THE **VILLAGE VOICE** TOWARD FRED.

WHO ARE THESE CATS AGAIN?

THE TALKING HEADS!

LIKE ALL OF O'BRIEN'S CLOSEST FRIENDS, FRED AND JEAN-MICHEL APPEAR REGULARLY ON HIS PUBLIC-ACCESS SHOW, THE CHAOTIC **TV PARTY**.

THIS IS YOUR EMERGENCY BROADCAST NETWORK...

ONE OF FRED FAB FIVE'S MOST MEMORABLE APPEARANCES WAS ON A **HALLOWEEN**-THEMED EPISODE.

I WAS JUST GETTING HIGH WITH PAUL NEWMAN...

NICKEL BAG

GUITARIST **CHRIS STEIN** IS THE CO-HOST OF TV PARTY AND CO-FOUNDER OF THE PUNK/NEW WAVE BAND **BLONDIE**. CHRIS AND **DEBBIE HARRY** BECOME FAST FRIENDS WITH FRED.

FAB FIVE FREDDY...

... MEET THE CLASH.

BLONDIE SOON RELEASES "**HEART OF GLASS**," WHICH LAUNCHES THE BAND INTO THE INTERNATIONAL SPOTLIGHT. FRED CAN'T BELIEVE HIS PALS ARE NOW **WORLD FAMOUS**.

MAKING IT HOME FOR A BIT WHILE OFF **TOUR**, CHRIS AND DEBBIE TAKE FRED UP ON HIS OFFER TO CHECK OUT THE **HIP HOP** SCENE IN THE BRONX.

THIS ONE FUH YOU, **PATTY DUKE!**

HA HA!

FROSTY FREEZE

AWARE THAT HIS FRIENDS HAVE LIMITED TIME, **FRED** MAKES SURE TO SHOW THE COUPLE **ONLY** THE BEST OF THE **BEST**.

THE **MERCEDES LADIES** ARE DEF, BUT, YOU'RE ABOUT TO SEE SOMETHING **SPECIAL**...

FLASH IS FAST!

FLASH IS COOL!

FREDDY, THIS IS SUCH A VITAL ART-FORM!

...NO DIFFERENT THAN PUNK ROCK!

ON THE RIDE BACK DOWNTOWN...

DEBBIE, YOU GUYS NEED TO MAKE ME A **STAR** AND CREATE A SONG ABOUT ME.

OH FREDDY! HA HA HA!!

WHAT THE FUCK YOU MEAN YOU MAKIN' A REKKID? YOU AIN'T NO EMCEE!!

CRAZY, RIGHT?

BIG BANK HANK

LET ME USE YOUR **RHYME BOOK**. WE'LL BE ABLE TO IMPRESS MISS SYLVIA.

THEN YOU'LL PUT US DOWN WITH HER?

I **AM** YOUR MANAGER.

HOW'D THIS EVEN HAPPEN?

" I WAS AT **WORK** JUST DOING MY THANG. PROB'LY **RECITING** YER OLD SUPER- MAN ROUTINE."

...HE'S A **FAIRY**, I DO SUPPOSE...

...FLYIN' THROUGH THE AIR, IN PANTY- HOSE...

" **YOU KNOW** THAT'S **STILL** ONE OF MY **FAVORITES**."

...HE MAY BE **ABLE** TO FLY ALL THROUGH THE **NIGHT**, BUT...

...CAN HE ROCK A **PARTY** 'TIL THE EARLY LIGHT?

" IT WASN'T A BUSY DAY, BUT..."

WE WANT TO MAKE A **RECORD** WITH RAPPING ON IT.

" THEY WANTED **ME** TO RHYME OVER SOME **MUSIC**, BUT MY TAPE PLAYER GOT SAUCE IN IT."

THIS FUCKED UP, HANK!

YA GOTTA GO.

CLOSED

CLICK

" MISS SYLVIA GOT A **DEF** BUCKET, BY THE WAY."

♪ I'M THE C-A-S-♫! A, THE N-O-V-A, AND THE REST IS F-♭♭ ♪ P L-Y... ♫ ♫

"YOU COULD **TELL** HER MIND WAS **SPINNING**."

I REALLY, **REALLY**, LIKE THE WAY IT SOUNDS WHEN YOU **RAP** OVER THIS **GOOD TIMES** SONG.

"I GUESS WE WAS MAKING A **RUCKUS** WHEN THIS CAT CAME UP TO US STRAIGHT OFF THE **STREET**."

I CAN RAP, TOO!

GET IN!

"SO THEN IT WAS JUST **ME** AND **MASTER GEE** BATTLING RHYMES BACK AND FORTH."

MY **NAME** IS KNOWN ALL OVER THE WORLD BY **ALL** FLY LADIES AND THE PRETTY **GIRLS**...

...I'M GOING DOWN IN HISTORY, I'M THE **BADDEST**...

"AIN'T NO QUESTION WE WAS **BUTTER** TOGETHER."

HO-TEL, MO-TEL, UH WHAT YUH GONNA DO TODAY?

SAY WHA?

"ONE OTHER BROTHER HAD THE COURAGE TO STEP UP."

3 GUYS MIGHT NOT BE NECESSARY. NOT SURE...

"ALL **3** OF US WENT BACK TO MISS SYLVIA'S AND IT BECAME CLEAR THAT **WONDER MIKE** WAS VALUABLE."

LIKE A CAN OF **BEER** THAT'S SWEETER THAN **HONEY**, LIKE A MILLIONAIRE THAT HAS NO **MONEY**...

LIKE A RAINY DAY THAT IS NOT **WET**, LIKE A **GAMBLIN'** FIEND WHO DOES NOT **BET**.

"I TOLD YOU IT WAS ALL **CRAZY**!"

OKAY! ALL THREE OF YOU ARE **MARRIED** NOW. WE'RE ABOUT TO START A NEW RECORD LABEL CALLED **SUGAR HILL RECORDS**, AND WE'RE CALLING YOU THE **SUGARHILL GANG**!!

SO, **NOW**, I NEED SOME GREAT RHYMES TO PUT ON WAX.

NO PROB. TAKE WHATEVER YOU WANT. ONCE ME AND **THE BROTHERS** GET WHERE WE NEED TO, MAKE **SURE** YOU PUT US DOWN WITH HER. OKAY?

GRANDMASTER CAZ →

OR, GMC!

THE **FATBACK BAND** BRINGS IN A LITTLE-KNOWN YOUNG EMCEE NAMED **TIM WASHINGTON** TO DO HIS THING ON TOP OF THEIR SONG, **CATCH THE BEAT.**

STRONG AS AN OX...

...TALL AS A TREE...

BILL CURTIS LIKES THIS NEW APPROACH SO MUCH THAT HE RENAMES THE SONG **KING TIM III** (PERSONALITY JOCK), AFTER THE RAPPER, WHOSE STYLE IS A MIX BETWEEN **DJ HOLLYWOOD** AND THE JOCKS ON BLACK RADIO.

SLAM DUNK, DO THE JERK...

...LET ME SEE YOUR **BODY** WORK!

THE RECORD COMPANY NOTICES THE COMPARISON TO RADIO DJ'S AS WELL.

THE JOCKS ARE GONNA BURY IT!

THEY'RE GONNA THINK YOU'RE MAKING FUN OF THEM!

NOT QUITE WHAT THE FATBACK BAND HAD IN MIND, THE SONG IS RELEASED AS A **B-SIDE** OF ANOTHER SINGLE, "**YOU'RE MY CANDY SWEET.**"

TO THE RECORD COMPANIES' SURPRISE, THE UNIQUE NEW TRACK GETS MORE RADIO PLAY **AND** CHARTS HIGHER THAN FATBACK'S **A-SIDE.**

WE GOTTA TREAT FOR Y'ALL HERE ON THE **DISCO SHOWCASE!**

THE RELEASE OF THE SONG PROVES THAT THE RADIO LISTENER IS AT LEAST **WILLING** TO PUT-UP-WITH **RAPPING** ON A RECORD. **KING TIM III** BECOMES A MOTIVATING CATALYST.

SYLVIA ROBINSON

WE NEED TO GET A MOVE-ON, NOW!

ROBERT "ROCKY" FORD

RUSSELL, CAN YOU GET ME EDDIE CHEBA ON THE PHONE?

YOU'RE **THTILL** ON THAT **EDDIE CHEBA** TIP? COME CHECK OUT **KURTITH BLOW** TOMORROW NIGHT AND WE'LL TALK.

RUSSELL SIMMONS KNEW THAT KURTIS BLOW WOULD BE A SMASH THIS NIGHT WITH **GRANDMASTER FLASH** CUTTING RECORDS BEHIND HIM. THE **FURIOUS FIVE** ARE NOWHERE TO BE FOUND.

SOMEBODY **SCREAM** !!!

FLASH

AS SIMMONS PREDICTED, FORD DECIDES TO CUT A **DEMO** WITH BLOW.

I KNOW A GUY WHO PRODUCED **CHRISTMAS** SONGS FOR **PERRY COMO**. IT WAS LIKE PRINTING MONEY.

ROCKY FORD SHARES HIS IDEAS WITH **JB MOORE**, A FELLOW BILLBOARD MAGAZINE DISSIDENT.

THERE WILL BE LESS OF A BARRIER TO ENTRY WITH A CHRISTMAS RECORD. A **LABEL** MIGHT EVEN **OVERLOOK** THAT IT HAS RAPPING ON IT.

J.B. LEFT BILLBOARD TO WORK ON A NOVEL, BUT BEFORE DOING SO...

J.B. MOORE SENT ME A **GREAT** SET OF LYRICS FOR KURTIS TO WORK FROM... A **PARODY** OF **THE NIGHT BEFORE CHRISTMAS**.

FORD AND MOORE COMBINE RESOURCES, HIRING **LARRY SMITH** TO CREATE THE MUSIC THAT KURTIS WILL BE RAPPING OVER.

GIVE US A FUNKY BASS-LINE LIKE **GOOD TIMES**.

SIMMONS INSISTS THAT THE DEMO CONTAINS A **B-SIDE** CONTAINING LOTS OF ORIGINAL KURTIS BLOW MATERIAL.

SOMEBODY SCREAM!

WHO'S HE TALKIN' TO?

IT'S A **HIP HOP** THING.

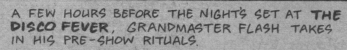

A FEW HOURS BEFORE THE NIGHT'S SET AT **THE DISCO FEVER**, GRANDMASTER FLASH TAKES IN HIS PRE-SHOW RITUALS.

NO ONE ELSE SHOULD REALLY BE HERE YET, LET ALONE THE **EMCEES**, WHO ALMOST ALWAYS **BARELY** MAKE IT IN TIME.

..THE HIBBY TO THE HIP HIP HOP AND YA DON'T STOP!

COWBOY?

..WHAT YOU HEAR IS NOT A TEST, I'M RAPPIN' TO THE BEAT...

?

..I AM WONDER MIKE AND I'D LIKE TO SAY "HELLO"...

DISCO FEVER

HUH?

NEXT ON THE MIC, IS MY MAN HANK, SO COME ON...

SUGAR HILL HAS TROUBLE GETTING THEIR FLAGSHIP RECORD SOME AIRPLAY, BUT **MR. MAGIC** IS HAPPY TO OBLIGE.

...YOU NEVER HEARD NOTHING LIKE THIS...

..."RAPPER'S DELIGHT."

WHBI

IN **FLATBUSH** A YOUNG LAWRENCE PARKER IS BOTH GLUED TO THE RADIO, AND TESTING HIS MOTHER'S PATIENCE.

...TONS OF FUN, AND I DRESS TO A TEE...

YOU'RE STILL AWAKE?!

BUT, MR. MAGIC'S DEF, MA!

HIS BROTHER'S NAME IS KENNY.

THAT'S "KENNY PARKER".

GRANDMASTER FLASH

WHO ARE THESE GUYS? I KNOW EVERYBODY! IT AIN'T BAMBAATAA. IT AIN'T BREAKOUT...

AFRIKA BAMBAATAA

THEY GONNA KILL THE CULTURE WITH VINYL!

RAHIEM, MELLE MEL

GARBAGE! THAT "IMP THE DIMP" ROUTINE IS ALL MINES!

AXE MURDERED THE SHIT!

DJ DISCO WIZ

HANK AIN'T NO EMCEE...

BILL ADLER

WHAT'S AMAZING IS THAT THEY'RE STARTING TO PLAY THE FULL 15-MINUTE SONG ON THE RADIO!!

BOSTON HERALD MUSIC CRITIC

WRITES A PIECE ABOUT THE "DISCO FEVER" IN PEOPLE MAGAZINE

CARLTON RIDENHOUR

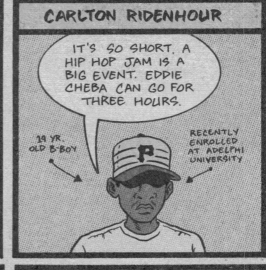

IT'S SO SHORT. A HIP HOP JAM IS A BIG EVENT. EDDIE CHEBA CAN GO FOR THREE HOURS.

19 YR. OLD B-BOY

RECENTLY ENROLLED AT ADELPHI UNIVERSITY

LOVEBUG STARSKI

...COULD HAVE BEEN ME, COULD HAVE BEEN ME, COULD HAVE BEEN...

RUSSELL SIMMONS

I RETHENT IT! THE DOE ITH CLOTHED BEFORE IT EVER OPENED!

BOBBY ROBINSON

I SELL THAT "RAPPER'S DELIGHT" FASTER THAN I GET THEM IN THE STORE. DIDN'T SEE THAT ONE COMING.

YO, CAZ! I HEARD YOU ON THE RADIO, MAN! BANANAS!!

WASN'T ME...

BUT, THEY WAS SAYIN' YO' RHYMES! I KNOW YOU GETTIN' PAID!!

DON'T YOU GOT SOMEWHERE TO BE?

MOTHER FUCK HANK!!

MINUTES BEFORE **PAUL WINLEY** STOPS INSIDE OF **BOBBY'S HAPPY HOUSE RECORDS**, THE OWNER, **BOBBY ROBINSON**, SOLD OUT OF "RAPPER'S DELIGHT" AGAIN! NO STORE IN NEW YORK CITY CAN KEEP THAT RECORD IN STOCK FOR VERY LONG.

THAT OUGHTTA LETCHA KNOW! THIS **RAPPING** ON RECORDS IS THE NEXT **DOO WOP**, BOBBY!

WHAT YOU GOT THERE?

PRESSED A NEW RECORD I MADE WITH MY DAUGHTERS, PAULETTE AND TANYA. "**RHYMIN' AND RAPPIN.**" IT'S GONNA MAKE YOU SOME MONEY!

'ZAT SO? WILL YOU DO CONSIGNMENT? THIS RAP SHIT COULD JUST BE A FLUKE!

IN THE MIDDLE OF **INTENSE** NEGOTIATION, ROBINSON'S NEPHEW, **SPOONIE GEE**, BURSTS INTO THE SHOP.

UNCLE BOBBY! CHECK IT OUT!

I MADE A RECORD!

YOU TOO?

WHAT THE HELL IS GOING ON?

I HOOKED UP WITH THAT PRODUCER PAL OF YOURS!

YOU AND YOUR FRIENDS IS CRAZY! WHATCH Y'ALL CALL YOURSELVES AGAIN? **THE TERRIBLE THREE**?

THE **TREACHEROUS THREE**. THIS RECORD IS ALL ME, THOUGH. IT'S CALLED **SPOONIN' RAP**.

41

SPOONIE ISN'T SURE HOW THE REST OF THE TREACHEROUS THREE WILL RESPOND, **BUT** HE KNOWS HE **BEST** SHARE THE NEWS BEFORE **MR. MAGIC** PLAYS THE RECORD ON THE RADIO.

YA SAY ONE FOR THE TREBLE, TWO FOR THE TIME, C'MON Y'ALL...

KOOL MOE DEE

WE COULD HAVE BEEN THE FIRST LEGIT GROUP ON WAX!?

L.A. SUNSHINE

I'M SAYIN'... THE RECORD IS **BUTTER**, BUT WHAT NOW? WE SPOONIE GEE AND THE TREACHEROUS **TWO**?

NAW! THAT WON'T WORK!

C'MON, Y'ALL. YOU KNOW I CAN'T BE ON **STAGE** BY MYSELF...

THINK **SPECIAL K** WOULD BE **DOWN** WITH THE CREW?

MAINTAINING A **FRIENDSHIP** WITH SPOONIE GEE, THE NEW **TREACHEROUS THREE** SEEM EVEN STRONGER THAN BEFORE AND THEY'RE ON A **QUEST** TO TAKE ON ALL COMERS.

FLASH AND THE FURIOUS IS TOO SCARED TO BATTLE US!!!

SPECIAL K

KOOL MOE

LEVERAGING THE **NEWFOUND** SUCCESS OF THE SUGARHILL GANG'S **RAPPER'S DELIGHT**, ROCKY FORD TAKES **KURTIS BLOW'S** DEMO TO EVERY MAJOR LABEL IN NEW YORK.

WE'LL CALL YOU...

$10,000 IN THE HOLE, ROCKY NEEDS TO MAKE A DEAL WITHIN THE MONTH FOR THEIR **SEASONAL** RECORD TO BE OUT BY **X-MAS**.

RUSSELL, MAN, HOW ARE THINGS LOOKIN'?

I HATE TO BE THE BEARER OF BAD NEWTH, KURTITH...

DUST

THE MEASURING STICK OF SUCCESS IN **HIP HOP** STARTED WITH **DJ'S** JUST THROWING GOOD PARTIES. THEN THE **DECIBEL** LEVEL AND RECORD SELECTION BECAME PARAMOUNT.

FLASH! GOTTA TALK TO YOU, MAN!

WHEN THE **MC'S** MOVED FROM BEHIND THE DJ, TO THE FOREFRONT, THEY BECAME **DOMINANT**. NOW, THOUGH...

we made a record...

?

GETTING YOUR VOICE ON **VINYL** HAS CAPTURED EVERYONE'S IMAGINATION, INCLUDING **THE FURIOUS FIVE**, WHO JUMPED AT A CHANCE TO FOOL AROUND IN A REAL RECORDING STUDIO.

IT'S FUCKED UP MAN! THEY MADE IT WITHOUT OUR PERMISSION!

WE DIDN'T SIGN NOTHIN'! THEY CHANGED THE NAME OF OUR GROUP!

THE PRODUCERS CHANGED THEIR NAME TO "**THE YOUNGER GENERATION**" AND THE RECORD IS CALLED "**WE RAP MORE MELLOW**."

ALL THE OTHER MC'S STEP TO THE REAR, 'CAUSE THE SOUND THAT YOU HEAR STEPS TO YOUR EAR...

BOBBY ROBINSON STILL DOESN'T UNDERSTAND THE RAP GAME, **BUT** HE COMPLETELY IS AWARE OF HOW MANY UNITS ARE MOVING THROUGH HIS STORE **DAILY**. HE'S EVEN CONSIDERING USING HIS OTHER BUSINESS, THE **ENJOY RECORDS** MUSIC LABEL, TO CAPITALIZE OFF OF THIS NEW CRAZE.

PUMPKIN, I'M NOT QUITE SURE **WHERE** TO START.

ONE THING'S FOR SURE, THOUGH. I CAN'T HAVE **KIDS** RAPPIN' OVER RECORDS LIKE THEY DO IN THE **PARK**.

ERROL "PUMPKIN" BEDWARD IS AN ENERGETIC YOUNG DRUMMER WHO HAS COLLABORATED WITH ROBINSON ON NUMEROUS **MUSICAL** PROJECTS.

I'M GONNA WANT **YOU** AND YOUR **FRIENDS** TO LAY DOWN INSTRUMENTALS.

WHO ARE THE **BEST** EMCEES I SHOULD KNOW ABOUT, **ANYHOW**?

WELL...

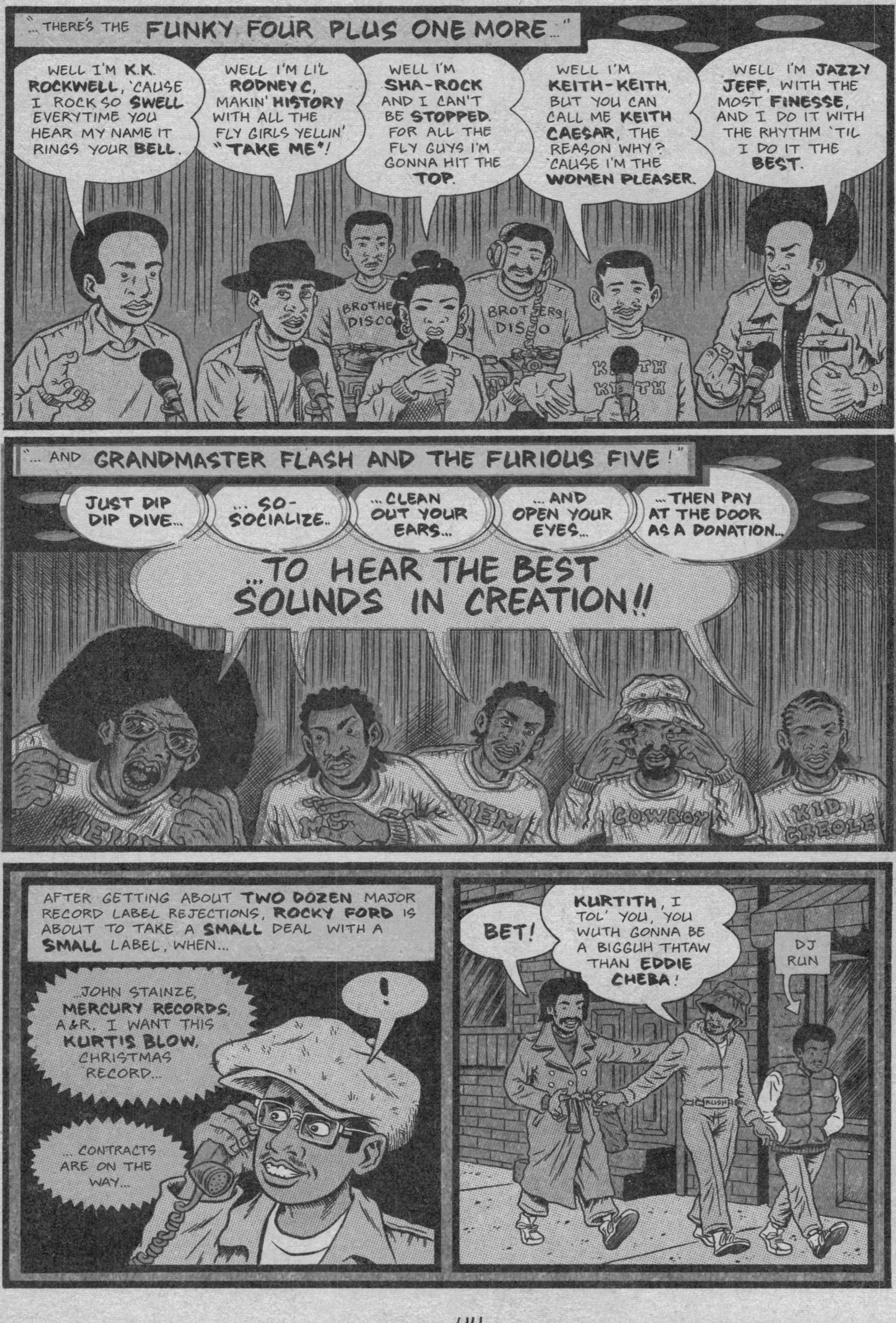
"...THERE'S THE FUNKY FOUR PLUS ONE MORE..."
WELL I'M K.K. ROCKWELL, 'CAUSE I ROCK SO SWELL EVERYTIME YOU HEAR MY NAME IT RINGS YOUR BELL.
WELL I'M LI'L RODNEY C, MAKIN' HISTORY WITH ALL THE FLY GIRLS YELLIN' "TAKE ME"!
WELL I'M SHA-ROCK AND I CAN'T BE STOPPED. FOR ALL THE FLY GUYS I'M GONNA HIT THE TOP.
WELL I'M KEITH-KEITH, BUT YOU CAN CALL ME KEITH CAESAR, THE REASON WHY? 'CAUSE I'M THE WOMEN PLEASER.
WELL I'M JAZZY JEFF, WITH THE MOST FINESSE, AND I DO IT WITH THE RHYTHM 'TIL I DO IT THE BEST.
"...AND GRANDMASTER FLASH AND THE FURIOUS FIVE!"
JUST DIP DIP DIVE...
...SO-SOCIALIZE...
...CLEAN OUT YOUR EARS...
...AND OPEN YOUR EYES...
...THEN PAY AT THE DOOR AS A DONATION...
...TO HEAR THE BEST SOUNDS IN CREATION!!
COWBOY
KID CREOLE
AFTER GETTING ABOUT TWO DOZEN MAJOR RECORD LABEL REJECTIONS, ROCKY FORD IS ABOUT TO TAKE A SMALL DEAL WITH A SMALL LABEL, WHEN...
...JOHN STAINZE, MERCURY RECORDS, A&R. I WANT THIS KURTIS BLOW CHRISTMAS RECORD...
!
...CONTRACTS ARE ON THE WAY...
BET!
KURTITH, I TOL' YOU, YOU WUTH GONNA BE A BIGGUH THTAW THAN EDDIE CHEBA!
DJ RUN
RUSH

REALIZING THE OPPORTUNITY TO RECORD AN ACTUAL GROUP WITH **CREDIBILITY** IN THE STREETS, BEFORE **SUGARHILL** HAS THE CHANCE, **BOBBY ROBINSON** OFFERS A DEAL TO THE **FUNKY FOUR PLUS ONE MORE.**

SOUNDS GOOD!

ALL OF US GOTTA ASK OUR **MOMS** FIRST, THOUGH...

KEITH KEITH

DETAILS ARE **MURKY** ABOUT WHETHER **DJ BARON** AND **DJ BREAKOUT** WILL BE PART OF THE DEAL. THEY **CERTAINLY** WON'T BE CONTRIBUTING MUSIC TO THE **RECORD.**

Y'ALL NAMES WILL BE ON THE RECORD, BUT, WE CAN'T HAVE YOU USING EXISTING MUSIC LIKE YOU DO AT YOUR PARTIES.

JIVE!!

WE GETTIN' ACED OUT...

WITHIN DAYS, THE GROUP LANDS IN THE STUDIO TO DROP **LYRICS** ON TOP OF THE **BEAT** THAT **PUMPKIN** (AND FRIENDS) LAID DOWN.

WHAT NOW?

JUST DO WHAT YOU **DO.**

SHA ROCK

IN ONE **FIFTEEN-MINUTE** TAKE, THE FUNKY FOUR PLUS ONE MORE PERFORM THEIR STAPLE **ROUTINES,** AND IN A WEEK'S TIME, THEIR VOICES ARE PRESSED INTO **VINYL.**

ENJOY RECORDS

#0000
Version "B"

Sweet Soul Music
EN 11029
Time: 14 Min.

RAPPIN AND ROCKING THE HOUSE
(K. Caesar / K. Smith / S. Green / J. Myree / R. Stone / B. Robinson)

Funky Four Plus One More
(Bros. Disco)
Music by Pumpkin & Friends
Produced by Bobby Robinson

33⅓ RPM

MOTIVATED BY HIS FIRST ACQUISITION FOR **ENJOY RECORDS,** ROBINSON SHOWS UP AT A **GRANDMASTER FLASH & THE FURIOUS FIVE** JAM... AND HE STICKS OUT LIKE A **SORE THUMB.**

THERE'S ONLY TWO EXPLANATIONS FOR WHY THAT **OLD-ASS** MAN IS HERE, AND I DON'T LIKE EITHER...

...IF HE AIN'T A **POLICE,** THEN HE'S LOOKING FOR HIS **DAUGHTER.**

DOO BAP! DAP BOOM BAP! BOOM! BOOM!!

FLASH 4

INTRODUCTIONS ARE MADE AFTER THE SHOW AND **CONTRACTS** ARE SIGNED PRETTY MUCH **ON THE SPOT.**

YOU KIDS ARE GONNA BE STARS!

LIKE THE **BROTHERS DISCO**, FLASH IS LEFT OUT OF PARTICIPATING IN THE ACTUAL MUSIC PRODUCTION.

...WHATCHOO MEAN, **FLASH**? BUT, YUH NAME'S ON THE **REKKID**!

YEAH, THEY KINDA **BOUGHT** MY NAME. IT'S **HARD** TO **EXPLAIN.**

GRANDMASTER FLASH AND THE FURIOUS FIVE GET ABOUT **$1200** EACH TO RECORD **SUPERAPPIN'** FOR **ENJOY RECORDS**. THERE'S AN ASSUMPTION THAT FLASH SPENDS HIS MONEY ON RECORDS. THE PEOPLE OF THE **BRONX** KNOW **EXACTLY** HOW THE **FURIOUS FIVE** USED THEIR CASH!

HYPERBOLE

ARTISTIC LICENSE...

...BUT THEY REALLY DID BUY DIRT BIKES WITH THEIR ADVANCE.

RAPPER'S DELIGHT IS A SUCCESS, SELLING OUT AT RECORD STORES ON A REGULAR BASIS, BUT NOW IT'S TIME TO SEE HOW THE **SUGARHILL GANG** GELS ON STAGE, IN FRONT OF A **LIVE** AUDIENCE.

MASTER GEE

THASS A LOTTA PEOPLE...

BIG BANK HANK

WONDER MIKE

DON'T WORRY! GROTTO HERE IS GOING TO RUN SECURITY.

IT JUST TAKES **MINUTES** TO REALIZE THAT SOME KINKS WILL NEED TO BE **WORKED OUT** FOR THEIR **CROSS-COUNTRY** TOUR TO GO SMOOTHLY. CROWD CONTROL AND SECURITY WILL BE A **PRIORITY**.

ONE OF THE SUGARHILL GANG'S NEXT STOPS IS IN **COLUMBIA**, **SOUTH CAROLINA**, WHERE A YOUNG SINGING GROUP CALLING THEMSELVES **THE SEQUENCE** IS PLANNING TO **BUM RUSH** THE BACKSTAGE IN SEARCH FOR A BIG BREAK.

YOU SURE?

YEAH, WE SHOULD MAKE A **RAP**!

CHERYL THE PEARL

BLONDY

ANGIE B.

ONLY A FEW RAP RECORDS HAVE MADE THEIR WAY TO SOUTH CAROLINA. **BESIDES** RAPPER'S DELIGHT, THE GIRLS ALSO HAVE **KING TIM III** AND AN **OBSCURE** RECORD BY **LADY B**, A RADIO DJ, WHO IS **PHILADELPHIA'S** ANSWER TO THE **RISING** POPULARITY OF **MR. MAGIC**.

TEC records

62   33-1/3 RPM
Time: 5:24

TO THE BEAT Y'ALL
(D. Clement & W. Clark)
"LADY B"
Publisher: M&A Publishing Co. ASCAP
Recorded at: Earmark Recording Studios, Phila., Pa.
Produced by: Andy Johnson for
King-Stewart Productions
Mixed by: Nick Martinelli

1228 SPRUCE ST PHILA PA 19107

THE GIRLS IN **THE SEQUENCE** TOOK A WEEK OR SO TO FINE TUNE THEIR ROUTINE BEFORE THE **SUGARHILL GANG** CAME TO TOWN. TONIGHT'S THE NIGHT, AND THE GANG DOES, IN FACT, COME WITH **MORE** AMPED-UP **SECURITY.**

Y'ALL BITCHES CAN SUCK MY

WHAT IS ALL THIS?

YOU SAY Y'ALL ARE **SINGERS?** LET'S HEAR WHAT YA **GOT!**

THE SUGARHILL GANG, AND BAND, WERE **SUPPOSED** TO BE ON STAGE **15 MINUTES** AGO, BUT **EVERYONE** WITHIN **EAR SHOT** IS JUST **MESMERIZED.**

FUNK YOU, RIGHT ON UP... GONNA FUNK YOU RIGHT ON UP... FUNK YOU...

OKAY, YOU'RE GONNA GO ON **STAGE** WITH THE **GANG.**

SURVIVING THEIR **TRIAL-BY-FIRE** WITH GREAT STYLE, THE SEQUENCE HEADS TO **NEW JERSEY.** WITHIN THE **WEEK,** THEY RECORD "FUNK YOU UP" FOR **SUGAR HILL RECORDS.**

A **MONTH** PASSES AND THEIR VINYL TRAVELS ALL ACROSS THE **COUNTRY,** INCLUDING THIS **COMPTON, CALIFORNIA,** BEDROOM, INHABITED BY A 14-YEAR-OLD MUSIC ENTHUSIAST NAMED **ANDRE YOUNG.**

RING DING DONG...

DRE!! TURN THAT SHIT DOWN !!!!

48

YES, **ROCKY FORD** SOLD **KURTIS BLOW'S** CHRISTMAS RAPPIN' TO A MAJOR LABEL, **MERCURY RECORDS**, BUT THE DEAL **ISN'T** LIFE-CHANGING IN TERMS OF THE ADVANCE PAYMENT. IT DOESN'T EVEN RECOUP ALL OF THE **PRODUCTION** COSTS.

WE'LL BE DOWN SOON, **MOMMA**...

...JUST GETTING MY **BOY** READY...

WHILE DRIVING WITH HIS FAMILY IN A **FUNERAL PROCESSION**, ROCKY BREAKS THE **SILENCE** BY TUNING IN TO THE POPULAR **FRANKIE CROCKER** ON WBLS.

THAT WAS NAT KING COLE'S CHRISTMAS SONG. NEXT...

AT THE SAME MOMENT, IN **HOLLIS, QUEENS**, RUSSELL SIMMONS WOULD LIKE TO IMBIBE **WITHOUT** GETTING HASSLED BY HIS **PARENTS** OR **BROTHERS**, FOR A CHANGE...

YO, RUSSELL!

THAT WAS NAT KING COLE'S CHRISTMAS SONG...

NOW THAT Y'ALL MADE A REKKID WITH **KURTIS**, WILL YOU PUT ME DOWN ON MY OWN **REKKID**?

...NEXT UP IS...

DJ. RUN

I TOLD YOU A **MILLION** TIME'TH! GET YUH **DIPLOMA** FIRTHT, AND WE'LL TALK.

...CHRISTMAS RAPPIN'" BY A NEW ARTIST, KURTIS BLOW...

ZENITH

CHRISTMAS RAPPIN' GOES ON TO SELL ABOUT **100,000** COPIES DURING THE **1979** HOLIDAY SEASON, AND THANKS TO THE **B-SIDE**, IT GOES ON TO SELL OVER **300,000** UNITS AFTER THE **NEW YEAR**.

FROM THE **LINCOLN PROJECTS**, THE ENIGMATIC **DISCO DAVE** AND **MIXMASTER MIKE*** ARE RESPONSIBLE FOR SOME OF THE BEST PARTIES IN **HARLEM**.

* **NOT** THE BEASTIE BOYS' MIXMASTER MIKE --ED

THEY SUPPLEMENT THEIR **INCOME** BY WORKING AT A COMMERCIAL RECORDING STUDIO DURING THE DAY.

...FOR JUST THIRTY CENTS A MONTH...

...SUCH A WASTE...

MIKE AND DAVE CAN **ALWAYS** COUNT ON A **POSSE** OF KUNG FU MOVIE-INFLUENCED **B-BOYS** KNOWN AS THE **POISON CLAN** TO SHOW UP AT JAMS. THEY YIELD ABOUT **30-40** PAYING CUSTOMERS... UNTIL MIKE AND DAVE PUT THEM TO **WORK** AS **ROADIES** AND **SECURITY**.

DON'T EVEN **LOOK** AT THESE SPEAKERS, SHADE-TREE **MUTHA-FUGGA**!

THE **BEST** EMCEES FROM WITHIN THE POISON CLAN—G.MAN, LA SHUBEE, BARRY BISTRO, E.K. MIKE C., AND REGGIE REG, ALONG WITH DJ DARYLL C.—BEGIN MAKING TAPES AND PERFORMING **ROUTINES** WITH THE HELP OF MIKE AND DAVE.

WE DON'T WANNA BE LEFT BEHIND, ALL WE WANNA DO IS JUST BLOW YOUR MIND, JUST ONE... MORE...TIME...

THEIR EARLY TAPES WOULD CONTAIN LOADS OF ENVIRONMENTAL **NOISE**. LOTS OF **ENGINES** REVVING, **TIRES** SCREECHING, AND **HORNS** HONKING.

HA HA! WE THE **CRASH CREW** OR SOMETHIN'!

SHH= BACK BY POPUL-Bzzz DEMAND SKREE- >ZaP=

THE **CRASH CREW'S** NAME STARTS TO RING OUT AROUND **BOROUGHS** OTHER THAN HARLEM... EVEN IN **AFRIKA BAMBAATAA'S** NEIGHBORHOOD.

KOOL DJ RED ALERT

THESE KIDS IS FROM WHERE?

ZULU

UNCHARACTERISTICALLY WITHIN THE CULTURE, **BAM** SHARES A HANDFUL OF HIS RECORDS WITH THE **CRASH CREW** AS AN ACT OF **PEACE, UNITY, LOVE,** AND **HAVING FUN,** THE **MANTRA** OF THE **ZULU NATION.**

THANKS, AFRIKA!

DJ DARRYL C

ZULU NATION

ONE OF THE **RECORDS** IS **FREEDOM'S** "GET UP AND DANCE."

WHAT IS THIS OTHER **SHIT**?

THE **PINK PANTHER** THEME?

THE CREW **IMMEDIATELY** HEADS TO THE COMMERCIAL STUDIO TO **LOOP** AND **SPLICE** THE FREEDOM **BREAK** 100 TIMES, OR SO, THEY CREATE AN **INSTRUMENTAL** TO RAP OVER AT PARTIES.

TEDIOUS BULL-SHIT, BUT, IT'LL **ROCK THE HOUSE!**

THIS NEW **AMMUNITION** FOR THE CRASH CREW WOULD CREATE A **DEATHBLOW** WHEN BATTLING OTHER GROUPS.

THEY **A'IGHT,** I GUESS...

KOOL MOE DEE

SPECIAL K

LA SUNSHINE

MIKE AND DAVE, BEING THE **ENTREPRENEURS** OF THE OUTFIT, DECIDE TO PRESS AN ACTUAL **RECORD** OF THE CREW'S INFAMOUS ROUTINE OVER THE FREE-DOM BREAK.

GIRLS, GIRLS GIRLS, GIRLS... GIRLS I DO **ADORE**...

FOR WHATEVER REASON, THEY CALL THE GROUP "**DISCO DAVE AND THE FORCE OF THE 5 MC'S**" AND THE TITLE OF THE RECORD IS "**HIGH POWERED RAP,**" WHICH THEY RUBBER STAMP ON THE VINYL'S **BLANK** WHITE LABEL.

WHO'D YOU SAY'S ON THIS **BOOTLEG**?

THE **CRASH CREW.** THEM DUDES OVER IN LINCOLN.

BETTER FOR YOUR HEAD...

IF YOU **WANT** THE RECORD, YOU HAVE TO GET IT STRAIGHT FROM THE **SOURCE.**

CAN YOU AFFORD THIS?

Let me hold three dollahs...

THE VINYL SOON MAKES ITS WAY TO **NEW JERSEY,** IN-TO **SYLVIA ROBINSON'S** POSSESSION.

HMMM... SOUNDS FUNKY...

COULD THE **SUGARHILL GANG** DO SOME-THING AS GOOD ON TOP OF THE SAME BEAT? HMM....

KURTIS BLOW'S *CHRISTMAS RAPPIN'* IS ACTUALLY RELEASED IN **EUROPE** AND BECOMES A **HIT** BEFORE IT GETS **IMPORTED** TO THE STATES. PART OF THE RECORD'S **SUCCESS** IS DUE TO BLOW'S LABORIOUS **EUROPEAN** TOURING SCHEDULE WITH HIS MANAGER, **RUSSELL "RUSH" SIMMONS.**

FIRST STOP: **HOLLAND**

HEY, KURTITH, CHECK OUT THITH GOOD **SHIT**!

MR. BLOW... MR. SIMMONS...

WHAT CAN **I** GET FOR **YOU**?

MITHTER THIMMONTH?

I'D LIKE THUM COCAINE AND THUM **PUTHY**!

"PUTHY," SIR?

PUTHY!

Y'KNOW, **VAGINA**!

IN **AMSTERDAM**, A RECORD COMPANY GUY TAKES THE **NEW YORK CITY** NATIVES TO HIS FAVORITE **MARIJUANA** BAR.

THIS IS **BUGGED OUT**!

DO YOU THINK THE **COPTH** ITH WATCHIN' UTH?

THEY GONNA BUTHT THITH PLAYTH ANY THECKOND.

EVERYBODY HERE SEEMS SO **HAPPY**.

53

IN FRANCE, THE BUSINESS MEN FROM **MERCURY RECORDS** TREAT THE **HIP HOPPERS** TO A **LAVISH** DINNER.

THIS STUFF DON'T EVEN EXIST IN **HARLEM**!

RELACKTH! TRY THUM **PRAWNTH**!

OUI OUI!

I DON'T KNOW, RUSSELL-MAN...

...MAYBE I'LL TRY SOME SHRIMP...

THEETH CLAMTH ITH **DEF**!
>slurp slurp<

WHERE CAN WE GET A BURGER?

THEY DON'T HAVE ANY **TJ SWANN** IN FRANCE, DO THEY?

Sniff...

Sniff

A FEW HOURS LATER, RIGHT BEFORE KURTIS IS TO HEAD OUT AND PERFORM...

RUSSELL-MAN, I TOLD YOU NOT TO EAT THEM MUSSELS...

BLARG

AS THEY MAKE THEIR WAY BACK TO THE STATES, IT'S APPARENT THAT BLOW'S TRANS-ATLANTIC **TOUR** HELPED GENERATE SOME **POPULARITY**.

...NAW, I NEVER BEEN TO THIS TOWN BEFORE...

WELCOME BACK TO OUR CATH'L...

ROCKY FORD SOON DECIDES TO TAKE ON THE **BURDEN** OF BEING KURTIS BLOW'S **ROAD MANAGER**.

...COLD BLOODED!

COME GET UTH! THEM **BITCHETH** EVEN TOOK OUR PANT'TH!

BOBBY ROBINSON'S RAP RECORDS WITH THE FUNKY FOUR PLUS ONE AND GRANDMASTER FLASH AND THE FURIOUS FIVE CONTINUE TO SELL INTO THE HUNDREDS OF THOUSANDS OF COPIES IN A FAIRLY SHORT TIME...

...COULD STILL JUST BE A FAD, THOUGH...

JUS' DON'T KNOW...

HE'S INSPIRED ENOUGH TO PRODUCE ANOTHER RECORD, BUT, NOT INSPIRED ENOUGH TO HUNT FOR NEW TALENT.

SPOONIE, YOU GONNA MAKE A RECORD WITH ME?

THOUGHT YOU'D NEVER ASK, UNCLE BOBBY!

FEELING TERRIBLE ABOUT DOING HIS FIRST RECORD WITHOUT HIS FRIENDS, THE TREACHEROUS THREE, SPOONIE GEE MAKES SURE THEY'RE INCLUDED THIS TIME.

HE SAID Y'ALL CAN DO WHATEVER Y'ALL WANT ON THE B-SIDE...

$300!

...A PIECE!

WORD!

ONCE AGAIN, PUMPKIN IS ENLISTED TO ARRANGE THE BEATS FOR THE NEXT ENJOY RECORDS MASTERPIECE.

ENJOY RECORDS

THE NEW RAP LANGUAGE
SPOONIE GEE
and the TREACHEROUS THREE
(with DJ Easy Lee)

33 1/3 RPM

FLASH AND THE FURIOUS AREN'T QUITE SURE HOW WELL THEIR ENJOY RECORD IS DOING, BUT THEY HAVE SOME IDEA AND THEY DON'T NECESSARILY LIKE IT.

FLASH WAS ON THE BEAT-BOX GOING...

...TAKE THE TRAIN, TAKE THE TRAIN...

MAKE, MAKIN' MONEY!!! HIT IT!!

GRANDMASTER FLASH AND CREW DECIDE TO PAY BOBBY ROBINSON A **VISIT** IN **HARLEM** TO SEE IF THERE **MAY** BE ANY **FINANCIAL DISCREPANCIES.**

WHERE OUR MONEY AT, BOBBY?

EVERYBODY GOT THE REKKID!!

!?

MAN, I'M SO BROKE!

MAKE THE SHIT RIGHT, BOBBY!

YOU OWE US MORE!

THE **62-YEAR-OLD** ROBINSON FOLDS UNDER **QUESTIONING...**

OH SHIT!

HE'S OUT COLD!

LUCKILY, THE NEAREST **HOSPITAL** IS PRETTY CLOSE, BY **FOOT.**

CONVENIENT, HUH?

SOUNDS LIKE HE'S SNORING!

FUCKIN' BOBBY...

AFTER A BIT OF **REHYDRATION...**

BOBBY, ARE YOU GONNA GIVE US ANY MORE MONEY?

NO RELATION TO BOBBY ROBINSON, **SYLVIA ROBINSON,** OWNER OF **SUGAR HILL RECORDS,** INTRODUCES HERSELF TO THE **FUNKY FOUR PLUS ONE** AFTER A SHOW.

DO Y'ALL THINK YOU'RE MAKIN' ENOUGH **MONEY** WITH **ENJOY RECORDS** ?

THERE'S NOT MUCH **RELIABLE** PROOF, BECAUSE **SUGAR HILL RECORDS** ISN'T REGISTERED WITH THE **RIAA**, BUT **RAPPER'S DELIGHT** SHOULD PROBABLY BE RAP MUSIC'S FIRST **GOLD** SINGLE.

WHY WOULD I OPEN UP MY BOOKS TO **ANYONE**?

SYLVIA ROBINSON CREATES HER OWN **GOLD RECORDS** AND **PLAQUES** FOR HER MUCH DESERVING **ARTISTS**.

THEY DON'T KNOW THE DIFFERENCE...

THANKS, MISS SYLVIA! MOMS IS GONNA **LOVE** THIS!!

SHE ALSO GIVES THE **SUGARHILL GANG** JUST ENOUGH **ROYALTIES** TO KEEP THEM FROM ASKING QUESTIONS WHILE SHE BUILDS A **WAR CHEST** FOR A VERY SPECIFIC **PURPOSE**.

I WANT YOU AND THE FURIOUS TO MAKE A RECORD FOR ME, **FLASH**.

YES!

I DON'T KNOW...

MELLE MEL

SENSING THE ARTISTS ON **ENJOY RECORDS** AREN'T HAPPY **FINANCIALLY**, SYLVIA HEADS **STRAIGHT** TO THE OWNER OF THE **LABEL** WITH A PROPOSITION.

BOBBY, YOU'RE NOT GIVING YOUR PEOPLE WHAT THEY **DESERVE**.

!

GRANDMASTER FLASH AND THE FURIOUS FIVE ARE TIRED OF IT! THE FUNKY FOUR PLUS ONE KNOW THAT THEY'RE BEING **SWINDLED**.

YOU AND I **BOTH** KNOW THIS **RAP** THING CAN EASILY BECOME THE NEXT **DISCO**. I'LL GIVE YOU $10,000 IF YOU LET THEM OUT OF THEIR **CONTRACTS**.

DONE!

THE BEST WAY TO REMEMBER THE PARADIGM SHIFT FROM **ENJOY RECORDS** TO **SUGAR HILL RECORDS** IS TO ILLUSTRATE HOW THE **FUNKY FOUR PLUS ONE** LOOKED IN THE BEGINNING...

... AND HOW THEY LOOK PERFORMING THEIR **DEBUT** WITH **SUGAR HILL**...

THAT'S THE JOINT!!

GRANDMASTER FLASH AND **THE FURIOUS FIVE** FROM THE **ENJOY RECORDS** ERA...

...AND **AFTER** SYLVIA'S NIECE, **DEBORAH JONES**, TOOK ARTISTIC LICENSE WITH THE GROUP WHILE ON SUGAR HILL.

SPOONIE GEE ALSO LEAVES ENJOY RECORDS FOR SUGAR HILL TO RECORD MONSTER JAM WITH THE LABEL'S FEMALE ACT, THE SEQUENCE.

THEY SAY ONE FOR TREBLE, TWO FOR THE TIME, C'MON GIRLS LET'S ROCK THIS...

SPOONIE HAS NOTORIOUS STAGE FRIGHT!

WHAM! BAM! THE MONSTER JAM! GET UP EVERYBODY AND DO THE FREAK TO THE BEAT!

BOBBY ROBINSON'S COMPANY STILL FLOURISHES WITH THE TREACHEROUS THREE MAKING FIVE STRONG-SELLING 12-INCH SINGLES FOR ENJOY.

FEEL THE HEARTBEAT...

FEEL THE HEARTBEAT...

WE'RE THE TREACHEROUS THREE...

WE GOT A NEW HEART-BEAT!

AS A FOLLOW-UP TO CHRISTMAS RAPPIN', KURTIS BLOW RECORDS THE BREAKS FOR MERCURY RECORDS IN THE SPRING, AND IT BECOMES THE DANCE HIT OF 1980.

YAY!!

THE FIRTHT GOLD REKKID IN HIP HOP HITHTORY!!

BET!

KURT

FREDERICK JAY RUBIN IS...

RICHIE RICK!

DON'T CALL ME FREDERICK!!!

SORRY, **SON**, I MEANT TO CALL YOU "**RICK**."

YOUR MOTHER SAID YOU LIKE TAKING PICTURES, **RIGHT**? WELL THIS IS NOW **YOURS** AND WE'RE EN-ROLLING YOU INTO A SUMMER **PHOTOGRAPHY** COURSE AT **HARVARD**!

FEH! I'M GOING **OUT**!!

?

THIS IS A **GREAT** SET OF WHEELS YOUR PARENTS GOT YOU, **RICK**!

I WANTED IT IN **BLACK**.

DO YOU HAVE THE STUFF?

$10!

WHO'S ON THIS ONE?

THE COLD CRUSH BROTHERS.

...BLACK PUNK ROCK!

NATURE ABHORS A VACUUM, AND **THE COLD CRUSH BROTHERS** HAVE FILLED A PROMINENT SPOT IN THE **SOUTH BRONX** CLUBS AND PARKS, WHILE THE **FUNKY FOUR** AND **GRANDMASTER FLASH** ARE BUSY TOURING AND MAKING RECORDS.

THE CHEBA HAWKS IS HAWKIN'!

THE STICK-UP KIDS IS STALKIN'!

WITH THE PRICE OF TRANSPORTATION NOW...

IT'S CHEAPER TO BE WALKIN'.

THE **BROTHERS DISCO'S** FORMER SOUND-MAN, **TONY TONE**, AND THE PUERTO RICAN **DJ CHARLIE CHASE** ARE RESPONSIBLE FOR THE **CUTTING** AND THE **SCRATCHING**.

TONY TONE, HE'S GONNA TAKE A FLY GIRL HOME.

CHARLIE CHASE, WITH THE FUNKY BASS!

Boo!

GRANDMASTER CAZ TAKES CENTER STAGE AS ONE OF THE FOUR EMCEES, ALONGSIDE **EASY A.D.**, **JDL**, AND **ALMIGHTY KAY G**.

Y'ALL IS PLAYED OUT!

THE **LIVE** PERFORMANCE IS **INTEGRAL** TO THE COLD CRUSH, AND THEIR MOST **POPULAR** ROUTINES ARE FEATURED ON **BOOTLEG'S**, AND CAN'T REALLY BE **REPRODUCED** ON AN ACTUAL **RECORD**.

WHO SAID THAT?

POINT HIM OUT!

GET 'IM CAZ!

EACH AND EVERY TIME WE PUT THE MUSIC **ON**, OR TURN IT DOWN FOR A SECOND TO MAKE YOU SAY "**HO**." SOMEBODY SOMEWHERE DEEP INSIDE THE **CROWD** HAS TO MAKE A COMMENT, OR SNAP OUT **LOUD**. NO MATTER WHERE WE ARE, NO MATTER WHAT WE **PLAY**, THERE'S ALWAYS A KNUCKLE-HEAD WITH SOMETHIN' TO **SAY**. SINCE WE'RE ON THE SUBJECT, I THOUGHT I'D **MENTION**, A LI'L SOMETHIN' TO YA. YOU WANT **ATTENTION**?

PAY 5 OR 6 DOLLAHS TO GET **INSIDE**, NO GIRL WANTS YA UGLY ASS SO YA SIT AN' **HIDE**. WAIT FO' AN OPPORTUNITY TO SCREAM OUT "**BOO**." THEN, LEAVE LIKE A SUCKA WHEN THE JAM IS **THROUGH**. GO HOME AN' TELL YA FRIENDS THAT THE PARTY WAS **WACK**, NEXT WEEK WE GOT YA MONEY 'CAUSE YA CAME RIGHT **BACK**!!

BUT, THIS TIME, **HA**! YOU BROUGHT YO' GIRL-FRIEND **TOO**, BUT, THE BITCH IS STANKIN' UGLY EVEN WORSE THAN **YOU**!!!

HA! I LOVE THIS ONE!

HEY!

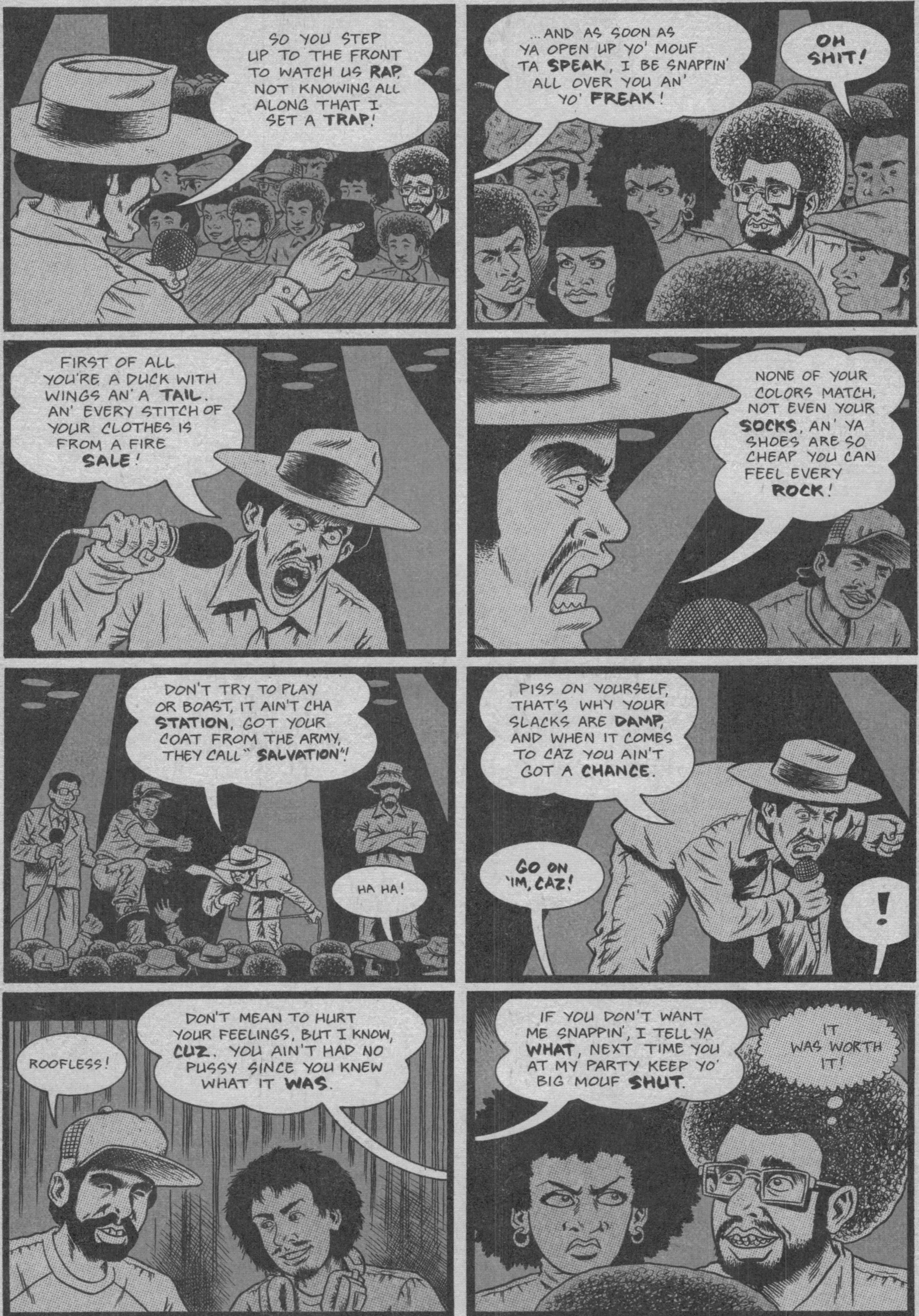
SO YOU STEP UP TO THE FRONT TO WATCH US RAP, NOT KNOWING ALL ALONG THAT I SET A TRAP!
...AND AS SOON AS YA OPEN UP YO' MOUF TA SPEAK, I BE SNAPPIN' ALL OVER YOU AN' YO' FREAK!
OH SHIT!
FIRST OF ALL YOU'RE A DUCK WITH WINGS AN' A TAIL. AN' EVERY STITCH OF YOUR CLOTHES IS FROM A FIRE SALE!
NONE OF YOUR COLORS MATCH, NOT EVEN YOUR SOCKS, AN' YA SHOES ARE SO CHEAP YOU CAN FEEL EVERY ROCK!
DON'T TRY TO PLAY OR BOAST, IT AIN'T CHA STATION, GOT YOUR COAT FROM THE ARMY, THEY CALL "SALVATION"!
HA HA!
PISS ON YOURSELF, THAT'S WHY YOUR SLACKS ARE DAMP, AND WHEN IT COMES TO CAZ YOU AIN'T GOT A CHANCE.
GO ON 'IM, CAZ!
!
ROOFLESS!
DON'T MEAN TO HURT YOUR FEELINGS, BUT I KNOW, CUZ. YOU AIN'T HAD NO PUSSY SINCE YOU KNEW WHAT IT WAS.
IF YOU DON'T WANT ME SNAPPIN', I TELL YA WHAT, NEXT TIME YOU AT MY PARTY KEEP YO' BIG MOUF SHUT.
IT WAS WORTH IT!

THE **COLD CRUSH BROTHERS** DISTRIBUTE TAPES OF THEIR LIVE PERFORMANCES AFTER THEY PLAY. ENDLESSLY BEING RE-COPIED AND PASSED AROUND, THE COLD CRUSH HELP TO **INSPIRE** A WHOLE NEW **GENERATION** OF EMCEE, LIKE YOUNG JOSEPH "**DJ RUN**" SIMMONS AND DARRYL "**EASY D**" McDANIEL, WHO BEGIN CREATING THEIR OWN **TANDEM** ROUTINES.

WE SHOULD GET **DAVY D** TO SCRATCH FOR Y'ALL.

EASY D AND DJ **RUN**! DUM DITTY DUM DITTY DITTY **DUM DUM**!

I DON'T KNOW ABOUT THITH "EETHY D" CAT...

THE ONLY IMMEDIATE **COMPETITION** TO THE COLD CRUSH ARE **GRANDWIZARD THEODORE'S** REFORMED VERSION OF THE **L BROTHERS**, NOW KNOWN AS THE **FANTASTIC FIVE EMCEES**.

ALL I HEAR IS "COLD CRUSH THIS" AN' "COLD CRUSH THAT"...

MAN, THE COLD CRUSH AIN'T SHEEEIT!

ON THE RECORD-MAKING SIDE OF HIP HOP, **SYLVIA ROBINSON** ISN'T HAPPY THAT SHE CAN'T CONVINCE THE INCREASINGLY POPULAR **CRASH CREW** TO JOIN **SUGAR HILL**. SHE DESPERATELY WANTS THE **STREET CRED** OF THEIR UNDERGROUND HIT, **HIGH POWER RAP**, WHICH USES VARIOUS **BREAKS** FROM **FREEDOM'S** "**GET UP AND DANCE**."

I NEED Y'ALL TO MAKE A TRACK THAT SOUNDS JUST LIKE IT.

GOT IT?

SKIP McDONALD (guitar)

KEITH LeBLANC (drums)

DOUG WIMBISH (bass)

THE SUGAR HILL HOUSE BAND'S **UNCANNY** REPLICATION IS FEATURED UNDER THE VOCALS OF **GRANDMASTER FLASH** AND **THE FURIOUS FIVE** ON THEIR **DEBUT** SUGAR HILL SINGLE, **FREEDOM**.

MELLE MEL RIGHT ON TIME, IT'S **TAURUS**, THE BULL, MY ZODIAC SIGN.

I'M **MR. NESS** AND I'M READY TO GO, AND I GO BY THE SIGN OF **SCORPIO**!

MY NAME IS **RAHIEM**, I DON'T LIKE TO FUSS, MY ZODIAC SIGN IS AQUARIUS.

THE **KID CREOLE** IS THE NAME OF MINE AND **PISCES** IS MY ZODIAC SIGN!

AN' I'M **COWBOY** AND I'M RUNNING THIS SHOW, MY ZODIAC SIGN IS... **VIRGO**!

EPISODE 336, SEPT. 27, 1980...

LET'S GET SOME HANDS TOGETHER, GANG, FOR MISTER **KURTIS BLOW!**

SOUL TRAIN

THESE... ...ARE... ...THE...

BREAKS!

REALIZING THAT THIS IS RAP MUSIC'S **FIRST** MAJOR PIECE OF NATIONAL TELEVISION EXPOSURE **KURTIS** ABSOLUTELY PERFORMS HIS **HEART** OUT, IMMEDIATELY GRABBING THE STUDIO AUDIENCE IN THE PALM OF HIS HAND. **DON CORNELIUS** HAS THIS TO SAY WHEN INTERVIEWING BLOW...

I MEAN IT DOESN'T MAKE SENSE TO OLD GUYS LIKE **ME...**

I MEAN, I DON'T UNDER- STAND WHY THEY LOVE IT SO MUCH.

...ha ha...

EPIC RECORDS DECIDES TO GET INTO THE GAME BY TAPPING A MAJOR SOURCE IN **HIP HOP, DJ HOLLYWOOD,** WITH A SINGLE CALLED...

...SHOCK, SHOCK THE HOUSE!

>FEH<

THE RECORD **FAILS** TO PICK UP MUCH STEAM, SO HOLLYWOOD HAPPILY GOES BACK TO HIS TRIED AND TRUE **NIGHTCLUB** GIGS.

OF ALL THE ANIMALS IN THE WORLD I'D RATHER BE A **SQUIRREL...**

...TO CLIMB UP UP ON THE HIGHEST MOUNTAIN AND =PTHHT= ALL OVER THE WORLD!

BUSY BEE STARSKI WAS AN EARLY MEMBER OF GRAND WIZARD THEODORE'S FANTASTIC FIVE EMCEES, CARRYING OVER FROM THE L BROTHERS, BUT BUSY IS PLAGUED BY THE SAME OBSTACLES THAT FORCED HIM TO LEAVE THE BROTHERS DISCO.

HOW IS WE S'POSED TO BE TAKEN SERIOUS, WITCHA MOMS GRABBIN' YOU OFF STAGE?

SHIT IS SILLY!

Y'ALL TRIPPIN'!

INDEPENDENTLY, BUSY BEE DOESN'T DO BAD FOR HIM-SELF, ESPECIALLY AFTER KOOL DJ AJ STARTS BACKING HIM MUSICALLY.

BAW WITTA BAW DANG DI-DANG DIGGY...

AJ'S ALWAYS PROMOTED GIGS AND RAP CONTESTS AROUND THE CITY. IT WON'T COME AS A SHOCK THAT BUSY BEE WINS ALL THE COMPETITIONS.

I'M TAKIN' OUT ALL BUMS!

I'M KNOCKIN' OUT ALL CHUMPS!

MONEY MONEY MONEY

MONEY MONEY MONEY

HELPED BY BUSY BEE'S AFFABILITY AND CHARISMA, HE, AJ, AND DJ SMALLS CATCH THE EAR OF BRASS RECORDS, THE SAME PRODUCERS WHO PUT OUT THE FURIOUS FIVE'S FIRST EFFORT, WE RAP MORE MELLOW.

MANY OF THOSE AJ/BUSY BEE "RAP CONTESTS" HAPPEN HERE. THIS VENUE IS ALSO WHERE SYLVIA ROBINSON FIRST WITNESSED LOVEBUG STARSKI, INSPIRING HER TO START SUGAR HILL RECORDS. OUTSIDE OF THE BRONX, THIS IS ONE OF THE ONLY OTHER GAMES IN TOWN.

HARLEM WORLD IS OWNED AND OPERATED BY A PLAYER KNOWN AS "FAT MAN." HE MAY OR MAY NOT HAVE DEEP UNDERWORLD CONNECTIONS. THERE ARE LOTS OF RUMORS FLOATING AROUND.

FAT MAN IS A PRETTY PHILANTHROPIC DUDE, HOUSING AND EMPLOYING MANY HIP HOPPERS WHO DON'T HAVE ANYWHERE ELSE TO GO.

AS RAP RECORDS CONTINUE TO CREEP OUT, FAT MAN DECIDES TO CHERRY PICK HIS BEST WORKERS AND SOME DYNAMIC RAP CONTESTANTS FOR A NEW VENTURE...

TAYSTER RECORDS

RAPPERS CONVENTION

Producer: Jack Taylor
TS 5400
STEREO 33½

SIDE A
Time 6'26"

WRITERS AND ARTISTS
HARLEM WORLD CREW

TWO CONTESTANTS INDUCTED INTO THE HARLEM WORLD CREW ARE THE VERY UNIQUE DOCTOR JECKYLL AND MR. HYDE.

ANDRE "DR. JECKYLL" HARRELL & ALONZO "MR. HYDE" BROWN BECAME AWARE OF HARLEM WORLD FROM ATTENDING CHARLES EVANS HUGHES HIGH SCHOOL WITH "RAPPING DJ" LOVEBUG STARSKI, WHO WAS ALREADY FUCKING ROYALTY.

THE FANTASTIC ALEEMS, A DUO OF ESTABLISHED FUNK MUSICIANS (and former roommates with JIMI HENDRIX) ARE EAGER TO PRODUCE A RAP RECORD.

THE MORE **POPULAR** DJS IN **NEW YORK** ALL HAVE SPECIAL RELATIONSHIPS WITH MANY STORE OWNERS.

"**RECORD**" **LENNY**? MR. **BAMBAATAA** SAYS YOU HAVE SOME STUFF FOR HIM TODAY.

AH, YES. SO YOU'RE **JAZZY JAY**?

JAZZY JAY IS A PRODIGAL **ZULU NATION** DJ, AND, YOUNGER COUSIN OF **KOOL DJ RED ALERT**.

BAM IS THE MASTER OF **REKKIDS**, NO DOUBT, BUT SOME OF THESE **REKKIDS** IS STRAIGHT **GAW-BITCH**.

HA HA HA!!

YOU NEED SOME **TRASH** REKKIDS TO PULL OFF THIS OLD **KOOL HERC** TRICK. 'SPECIALLY IF YOU WANNA BE MEAN ABOUT IT.

WHAT **KOOL HERC** TRICK?

JUST LIKE KOOL HERC USED TO DO, **AFRIKA BAMBAATAA** SOAKS HIS VINYL IN WATER SO THAT HE CAN EASILY **PEEL** THE LABELS OFF AND **MIX** THEM UP WITH DIFFERENT RECORDS.

NOT ONLY DOES THIS CAUSE **CONFUSION** WITH **RIVAL DJ'S**, BUT IT ALSO GETS THEM TO WASTE THEIR **MONEY**, IF THEY'RE HONEST FOLK.

MARY! MARY!

THIS BEAT IS **DEF**! SOME REKKID CALLED **KEN : BY REQUEST ONLY**.

WE GOTS TO COP THAT SHIT, FO' REAL!!

BAMBAATAA HAS BEEN BIDING HIS TIME, IN NO RUSH TO START MAKING **RECORDS**. IN THE MEANTIME, HIS **ZULU NATION** HAS AMASSED HANDFULS OF **EMCEES** INCLUDING **MR. BIGGS, POW WOW, ICE ICE, MC. G.L.O.B.E, SUNDANCE, HUTCH HUTCH, IKEY C, LISA LEE, MASTER ICE**, AND OTHERS...

PAUL WINLEY PRODUCES **VICIOUS RAP**, WITH HIS DAUGHTER, TANYA, RAPPING AGAIN. IT'S A **UNIQUE** RECORD IN THAT IT HAS A **GLIMMER** OF **SOCIAL RELEVANCE** BEYOND THE PARTY VIBE OF **EVERY** OTHER RELEASE, SO FAR.

SHE CALLS THE PIGS **"TURKEYS"** AN' SAYS SHE BEEN "ARRESTED FOR FIRST DEGREE **RHYMES**."

MAYBE THIS FRESH SCOPE HELPS EASE BAMBAATAA AND CREW INTO WORKING WITH **WINLEY**. BAM **DIVIDES** HIS EMCEE ROSTER INTO TWO GROUPS, THE **COSMIC FORCE** AND THE **SOUL SONIC FORCE** TO CREATE **ZULU NATION THROWDOWN VOL. 1** AND **2.**

ONE LAST THING... DID I MENTION YOU **CAN'T** USE EXISTING RECORDS TO MAKE THE **MUSIC?**

SAY WHA'?

!

BAMBAATAA **HATES** THE EXPERIENCE FOR **MANY** REASONS, INCLUDING LACK OF CREATIVE CONTROL ON THE **MUSICAL SIDE**, AND LACK OF **INCOME** ON THE **FINANCIAL SIDE**. BAM AND THE ZULUS **QUICKLY** GO BACK TO DOING WHAT THEY DO **BEST**.

ZULU!

GESTAPO!

AT THIS **ZULU JAM**, 2 ENTREPRENEURIAL **WHITE BOYS** WANDER IN AFTER A **YANKEE** GAME. ONE GUY IS **CORY ROBBINS**, A RECORD EXEC WHO MISSED OUT ON SIGNING **KURTIS BLOW**. THE OTHER IS **TOM "TOMMYBOY" SILVERMAN**, PUBLISHER OF **DANCE MUSIC REPORT**, WITH THOUGHTS OF STARTING A RECORD LABEL.

CORY? WHAT THE FUCK IS THIS?

IF YOU LISTEN TO **MEDGAR EVERS** COLLEGE RADIO STATION **91.5FM** AT THE RIGHT TIMES, YOU'RE IN FOR A **TREAT**.

YES, I'M SUPER-RHYMES, I'M **22**... I'M GONNA BE 100 BEFORE I'M **THROUGH**...

INTERMITTENTLY, A STUDENT, **JIMMY SPICER**, GETS ON THE MIC, WEAVING RHYTHMIC **TALES** OF GENIES, SUPERHEROES, ALIENS, AND MORE TO THE LISTENERS.

HAW!

...TRANSYLVANIA'S WHERE HE CALLS HIS **HOME**, UNTIL ONE DAY HE DECIDED TO **ROAM**...

THIS **UNIQUE** APPROACH OF **STORY-RHYMING** CATCHES THE ATTENTION OF A FEW **RECORD PRODUCERS** THAT JIMMY'S **MOTHER** HAPPENS TO KNOW. THE RESULT: **ADVENTURES OF SUPER RHYME**.

I INVENTED **HIP HOP**! I WAS THE **FIRST** TO RHYME ON **BEAT**!

I DID ALL THAT BACK IN **1974** WHEN MY NAME WAS **M.C. MOP**. THAT'S HOW LONG I BEEN IN **THIS**!

COOL AS SNOW!

SAVOIR-FAIRE!

THE RECORD IS AN **INFLUENTIAL** HIT ON THE STREETS OF **NEW YORK**, AND THIS ISN'T LOST ON **RUSSELL "RUSH" SIMMONS**, WHO'S BEEN LOOKING TO MANAGE MORE ACTS ON THE **HEELS** OF HIS **SUCCESS** WITH **KURTIS BLOW**.

JIMMY, WE GONNA MAKE YOU A **THTAW!** KEEP ROLLIN' WIF **RUSH**!

WE GONNA GETCHOO THUM **CLAWK WALLABEETH!**

BET!

ADVENTURES OF SUPER RHYME ALSO HAS AN **INSPIRING** EFFECT ON TWO YOUNG EMCEES AT THE **HIGH SCHOOL OF MUSIC AND ART**, DANA MCLEESE AND RICKY WALTERS, IN TANDEM KNOWN AS **THE KANGOL CREW**.

...JUST MAKE SURE YOU REMEMBER THE NAME! MR. **DANA DANE** WITH **FAME**!

...AND **M.C. RICKY D**, IN THE PLACE TO BE!

BALLY SHOES!

WE KICKIN' IT LIVE IN **1980**, FUH ALL THE **LADIES**, Y'UM SAYIN'? YA **CRUMBS** AN' **CRAB RAPPAHS!**

DON'T BITE HIS RHYMES UNLESS YOU'RE A BACK-STABBER!

FRESH DRESSED, LIKE A MILLION BUCKS!

SYLVIA ROBINSON AND THE SUGAR HILL LABEL ARE MANY THINGS, BUT STUPID ISN'T ONE OF THEM. THEY CONTINUE TO TRY AND TAP THE SUGARHILL GANG FOR FOLLOW-UP HITS, RELEASING RECORD AFTER RECORD. THEIR CLOSEST SUCCESS, AT THIS POINT, IS PROBABLY A JOINT CALLED "8TH WONDER."

WOO HAW! GOTCHA ALL IN CHECK!

EVERY WEEKEND, RICK RUBIN'S PARENTS BRING HIM INTO THE CITY SO THAT HE CAN SEE HIS FAVORITE BANDS PERFORM.

GABBA GABBA WE ACCEPT YOU...

...WE ACCEPT YOU, ONE OF US!

$50 MOSRITE GUITAR!

HIS FOLKS WAIT FOR HIM OUTSIDE UNTIL THE SHOW'S OVER. IF HE WERE TO DRIVE IN HIMSELF, HE'D HAVE TO RISK HIS FIAT BEING STOLEN.

YES, DEAR, FREDERICK SAID THE CONCERT PERFORMANCE SHOULD END AROUND 12:00.

CBGB
315 OMFUG 315

A NEW **RECORD** HAS BEEN POPPING UP HERE AND THERE IN **NEW YORK**. UNLIKE **EVERY** OTHER RAP RECORD IN EXISTENCE, THIS ONE DOESN'T COME FROM NYC OR THE **SUGAR HILL** LABEL. IT'S FROM **CONNECTICUT**, AND VERY **PROUD** OF IT.

RAPPIN' WITH MR. MAGIC IS THE BRAINCHILD OF **TONY "MR. MAGIC" PEARSON**, A NEW HAVEN-BASED DJ, WHO IS **PROBABLY** AWARE OF THE BEFUDDLEMENT HE'S GENERATING WITH **SOME** LESS-INFORMED **HIP HOP** FANS IN "THE APPLE."

GARBAGE!

HOW COULD HE DO THIS SHIT TO US? **BENEDIC' AWNOLD** MUTHA FUGGA!!

STANFORD! WE DOWN! NORWALK! WE DOWN! BRIDGEPORT! WE DOWN! NEW HAVEN! WE DOWN! ANSONIA! WE DOWN! HARTFORD! WE DOWN!

FUCK MISTER MAGIC!

IT'S ALSO WORTH NOTING THAT **PEARSON** IS **RESPONSIBLE** FOR THE NEW RECORD **GET UP** BY HIS 12-YEAR-OLD NEPHEW NICKNAMED **POOKIE BLOW**. MAYBE PEARSON'S **TRYING** TO ASSOCIATE THE BOY WITH **KURTIS BLOW**? MAYBE NOT?

SAY POOKIE BLOW, WHAT YA GONNA DO?

I'M GONNA PLAY THIS HERE **KAZOO**!

THE WELL-ESTABLISHED WHBI RADIO HOST, **MR. MAGIC**, ISN'T PHASED BY THIS **CONNECTICUT** COINCIDENCE, IN THE **LEAST**. HIS PROGRAM IS JUST MAKING HIM MORE AND **MORE** POPULAR, THUS MAKING HIM THE DE-FACTO **TASTE** MAKER OF THIS **NEW** RAP MUSIC **INDUSTRY**.

BEWARE OF CHEAP IMITATORS, Y'ALL!

JALIL, MR. MAGIC'S INTERN.

THE "**REAL**" MR. MAGIC AND OTHER **KEY** HIP HOP LUMINARIES ALL GET **V.I.P.** TREATMENT AT **SAL ABBATIELLO'S** BRONX NIGHTCLUB, THE **DISCO FEVER**. THIS GANG BECOMES AFFECTIONATELY KNOWN AS THE "**JUICE CREW**." MAGIC, BEING THE **GATEKEEPER** BETWEEN RAP RECORDS AND THE RADIO, IS DEEMED "**SIR JUICE**."

KURTIS BLOW | MELLE MEL | SWEET G. | MANDINGO | SAL ABBATIELLO | GRAND-MASTER FLASH | MISTER MAGIC

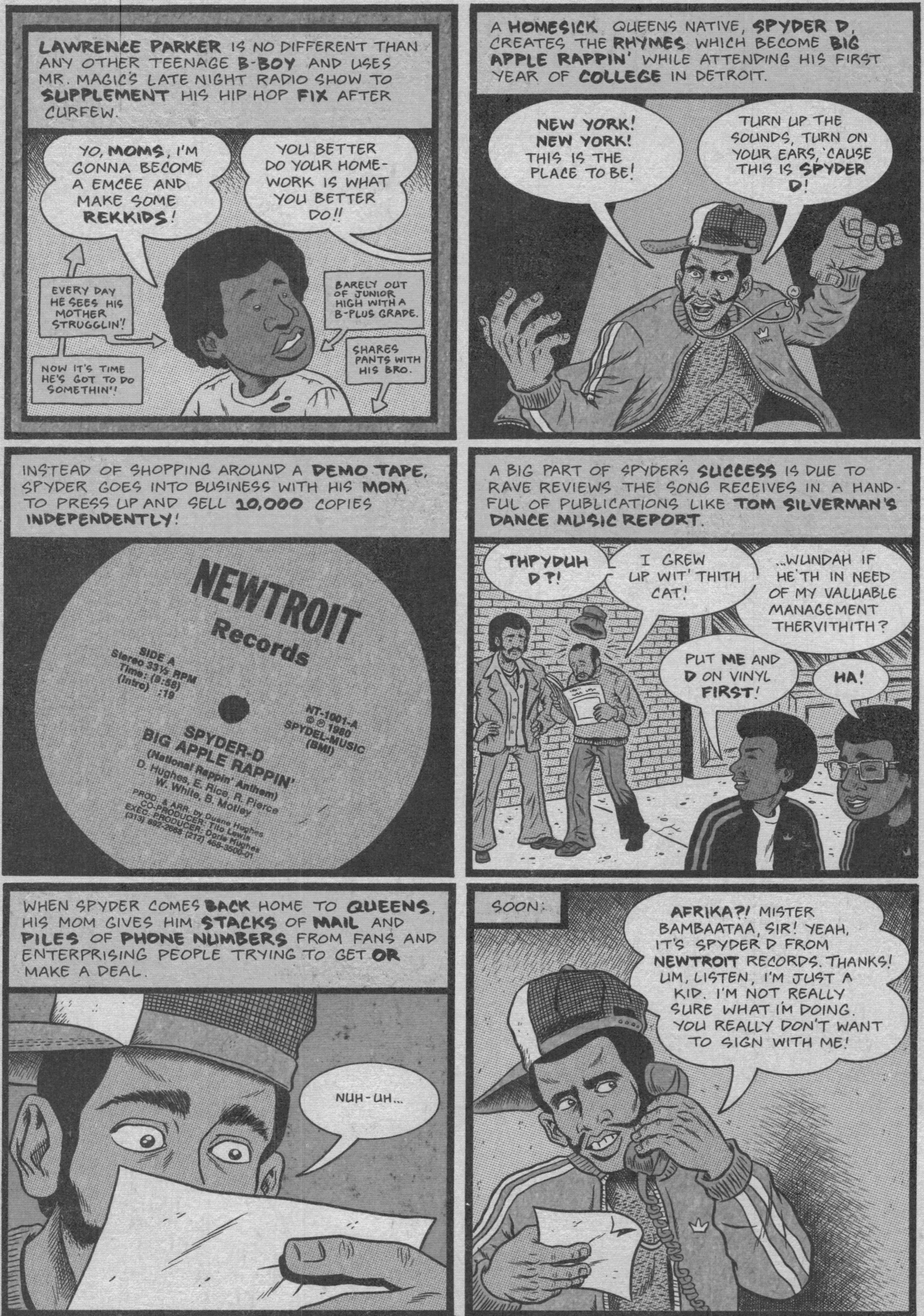
LAWRENCE PARKER IS NO DIFFERENT THAN ANY OTHER TEENAGE B-BOY AND USES MR. MAGIC'S LATE NIGHT RADIO SHOW TO SUPPLEMENT HIS HIP HOP FIX AFTER CURFEW.
YO, MOMS, I'M GONNA BECOME A EMCEE AND MAKE SOME REKKIDS!
YOU BETTER DO YOUR HOME-WORK IS WHAT YOU BETTER DO!!
EVERY DAY HE SEES HIS MOTHER STRUGGLIN'!
NOW IT'S TIME HE'S GOT TO DO SOMETHIN'!
BARELY OUT OF JUNIOR HIGH WITH A B-PLUS GRADE.
SHARES PANTS WITH HIS BRO.
A HOMESICK QUEENS NATIVE, SPYDER D, CREATES THE RHYMES WHICH BECOME BIG APPLE RAPPIN' WHILE ATTENDING HIS FIRST YEAR OF COLLEGE IN DETROIT.
NEW YORK! NEW YORK! THIS IS THE PLACE TO BE!
TURN UP THE SOUNDS, TURN ON YOUR EARS, 'CAUSE THIS IS SPYDER D!
INSTEAD OF SHOPPING AROUND A DEMO TAPE, SPYDER GOES INTO BUSINESS WITH HIS MOM TO PRESS UP AND SELL 10,000 COPIES INDEPENDENTLY!
NEWTROIT Records
SIDE A
Stereo 33⅓ RPM
Time: (5:58)
(Intro) :19
NT-1001-A
© ℗ 1980
SPYDEL-MUSIC
(BMI)
SPYDER-D
BIG APPLE RAPPIN'
(National Rappin' Anthem)
D. Hughes, E. Rice, R. Pierce
W. White, B. Motley
A BIG PART OF SPYDER'S SUCCESS IS DUE TO RAVE REVIEWS THE SONG RECEIVES IN A HAND-FUL OF PUBLICATIONS LIKE TOM SILVERMAN'S DANCE MUSIC REPORT.
THPYDUH D?!
I GREW UP WIT' THITH CAT!
...WUNDAH IF HE'TH IN NEED OF MY VALUABLE MANAGEMENT THERVITHITH?
PUT ME AND D ON VINYL FIRST!
HA!
WHEN SPYDER COMES BACK HOME TO QUEENS, HIS MOM GIVES HIM STACKS OF MAIL AND PILES OF PHONE NUMBERS FROM FANS AND ENTERPRISING PEOPLE TRYING TO GET OR MAKE A DEAL.
NUH-UH...
SOON:
AFRIKA?! MISTER BAMBAATAA, SIR! YEAH, IT'S SPYDER D FROM NEWTROIT RECORDS. THANKS! UM, LISTEN, I'M JUST A KID. I'M NOT REALLY SURE WHAT I'M DOING. YOU REALLY DON'T WANT TO SIGN WITH ME!

CHERYL LYNN'S 1978 DISCO HIT, **GOT TO BE REAL**, HAS AN INFECTIOUS **BREAK** THAT IS A STAPLE AT **HIP HOP** JAMS. IT DOESN'T TAKE LONG FOR THIS TO TRANSLATE ON **WAX**.

TO BE REALLLLLLLLL...

LISTER-HEWAN-LOWE, OWNER OF THE REGGAE LABEL **CLAPPERS RECORDS**, DECIDES TO PRODUCE A **SOCIALLY CONSCIOUS** RAP RECORD JUXTAPOSED AGAINST LYNN'S MORE **UPBEAT** MUSIC.

CLAPPERS RECORDS AREN'T MEANT TO BE ENTERTAINMENT...

...THEY'RE WEAPONS WITHOUT COMPROMISE!

THE RESULT, **HOW WE GONNA MAKE A BLACK NATION RISE**, BY **BROTHER D** (with COLLECTIVE EFFORT) DROPS ITS HEAVY-HANDED **MESSAGE** TO MANY **DEAF EARS**.

DAMN! LET'S EVEN THE SCORE 'CAUSE WE'RE FIRED UP AND WON'T TAKE IT NO MORE! WE'RE FIRED UP AND WON'T TAKE IT NO MORE...

THANKFULLY, IF THE **LYRICAL** CONTENT IS **LOST** ON LISTENERS, THE **ARTWORK** ON THE VINYL IS **STRONG** ENOUGH TO GET THE POINT ACROSS.

CARLTON DOUGLAS RIDENHOUR, A GRAPHIC DESIGN MAJOR AT ADELPHI UNIVERSITY, IS ONE OF THE FEW INITIAL **B-BOYS** THIS RECORD **RESONATES** WITH, BOTH **MUSICALLY** AND **VISUALLY**...

YO, **CHUCK**, YOU TRYIN' TO COME AND CHECK OUT **BLACK CAESAR** AT THE THEATER?

HEY, **DRÉ**, THAT'S AN IDEA I CAN ROLL WITH, **BUT**, I GOTTA FINISH THE POSTER FOR THE NEXT **SPECTRUM CITY** JAM.

DIB-BE-DIB-BE-DIZE, BUT, HOW WE GONNA MAKE A BLACK NATION RISE?

73

AFTER AGREEING TO MAKE A SOLO RECORD UNDER THE NAME **LONNIE LOVE**, **MR. HYDE** RECRUITS HIS PARTNER **DR. JECKYLL** TO HELP COME UP WITH SOME LYRICS.

SURE, I'M DOWN, **BUT**, YOU GOTTA PUT ME ON THE **NEXT** RECORD. COOL?

JECKYLL HAS AN ABILITY TO SPOT BUSINESS OPPORTUNITIES.

WHILE PRODUCING THE RECORD, **THE FANTASTIC ALEEMS** MAKE THE CHOICE TO USE **CHERYL LYNN'S** FAMOUS JOINT **UNDERNEATH** LONNIE LOVES VOCALS.

BE CAREFUL, LONNIE. DON'T TOUCH THE...

...MIKE WHEN YOU'RE PERFORMING YUH LYRICS.

CRAMMING THESE INGREDIENTS TOGETHER RATHER QUICKLY, THE SINGLE, **YOUNG LADIES**, IS RELEASED ON THE ALEEMS'S TINY LABEL, **NIA RECORDS**.

EVEN THOUGH I'M A MAN, **I MUST CONFESS!**

MEANWHILE, **CORY ROBBINS** AND HIS FRIEND **STEVE PLOTNICKI** EACH BORROW $17,000 FROM THEIR PARENTS TO CREATE THEIR OWN COMPANY, **PROFILE RECORDS**. COINCIDENTALLY, ROBBINS SIGNED THE ALEEMS TO THEIR EARLIER SUCCESS WHEN HE WAS AN **EXECUTIVE** AT PANORAMA RECORDS.

NOW THAT WE'RE PAYING RENT, **CORY**, WE BETTER MAKE A **PLAN!**

IT WAS AT **PANORAMA** WHERE ROBBINS MISSED OUT ON SIGNING **KURTIS BLOW**. NOW, WITH PROFILE RECORDS, CORY WANTS TO HIT THE GROUND RUNNING WITH A **RAP RECORD** TO CAPITALIZE ON THE NEW **FAD**. HE CALLS UP HIS OLD PALS, **THE FANTASTIC ALEEMS**.

SURE YOU CAN HAVE **YOUNG LADIES**...

...FOR $5500!

UM, DEAL...

PROFILE RECORDS **RERELEASES** YOUNG LADIES FOR THEIR FIRST EFFORT. IT BECOMES A **MINOR** HIT IN **FLORIDA**, BUT THAT'S ABOUT IT. ROBBINS AND PLOTNICKI ARE STARTING TO FEEL **DESPERATE**. MR. HYDE APPRECIATES THE CHANCES HE'S **EARNED**.

EVER THINK ABOUT JOINING THE **MILITARY**? SON, DO YOU KNOW WHAT A **QUOTA** IS?

25¢?

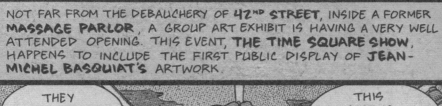

NOT FAR FROM THE DEBAUCHERY OF **42ND STREET**, INSIDE A FORMER **MASSAGE PARLOR**, A GROUP ART EXHIBIT IS HAVING A VERY WELL ATTENDED OPENING. THIS EVENT, **THE TIME SQUARE SHOW**, HAPPENS TO INCLUDE THE FIRST PUBLIC DISPLAY OF **JEAN-MICHEL BASQUIAT'S** ARTWORK.

THEY KEEP CALLING ME "**SAMO**."

THIS SHIT IS KIND OF ADDICTIVE!

FRED FAB FIVE IS A PART OF THE SHOW, AS WELL. HE ACTUALLY JUST FINISHED HANGING HIS PAINTING.

OH, I READ ABOUT THIS GUY, FRED, IN THE **VILLAGE VOICE**!!

YOU KNOW HE'S THE SAME GUY WHO PAINTED THAT **CAMPBELL SOUP** TRAIN!

THE **MTA** HAS LET THAT TRAIN RUN FOR **YEARS**. SOMEONE THERE MUST **LIKE** IT.

GRAFFITI, STREET ART, URBAN ART... WHATEVER YOU WANT TO CALL IT, IT'S THE MOST **VITAL** FORM OF EXPRESSION TODAY.

FRED!

!!!!

FREDDY, CAN YOU SIGN MY PRINT?

THIS PROBABLY ISN'T THE FIRST TIME **KEITH HARING'S** SHEER ENTHUSIASM CAUSES HIM SOME **EMBARRASSMENT** IN THE DOWNTOWN ART SCENE. HE'S BEEN IN **NYC** SINCE **1978** STUDYING AT THE **SCHOOL OF VISUAL ARTS**.

I'VE BEEN HEARING A LOT ABOUT YOUR WORK, TOO. THANKS!

FRED, CAN I BORROW YOU FOR A SEC. THAT FILMMAKER IS HERE!

CHARLIE AHEARN!

CHARLIE WHO?

CHARLIE **AHEARN.** YOU KNOW HIS MOVIE. WHATSACALLED? THE POSTERS ARE EVERY-WHERE. WITH THE **BLOODY** GUY.

"OH YEAH! THAT MOVIE'S BEEN PLAYING A LOT IN THE **L.E.S.**"

FRED **FAB FIVE,** MEET **CHARLIE AHEARN...**

CHARLIE, THIS IS THE GUY WHO KNOWS **LEE QUINONES.** THEY'RE GOOD PALS!

CHARLIE-MAN, WE'RE GONNA HAVE TO WORK TO-GETHER ON THIS PROJECT! THERE'S A **FLICK** THAT NEEDS TO BE MADE AND WE'RE THE **ONLY** ONES EQUIPPED TO MAKE IT ALL HAPPEN.

THIS... **ART...** THIS **GRAFFITI-**SHIT IS ONLY A PART OF IT. I GOT THIS **THEORY** THAT IT'S A PART OF A BIGGER **CULTURE.** THE EMCEES AND THE DJ'S HANDLE THE MUSICAL PART. THERE'S **FASHION** AND **DANCE.** IT'S ALL **HIP HOP** AND NEEDS TO BE PACKAGED TOGETHER ON THE **BIG SCREEN,** YA DIG?

UM, SO YOU KNOW **LEE,** RIGHT?

IF YOU BRING HIM BY TOMORROW, I'LL PAY YOU GUYS $50 EACH TO DO A MURAL ON THE FRONT OF THIS BUILDING.

SYLVIA ROBINSON CATCHES WORD THAT **THE CRASH CREW** IS HAVING TROUBLE WITH **MIX-MASTER MIKE** AND **DISCO DAVE** OVER MONEY.

I SET A MEETING UP WITH THE BOYS...

WHEN THE CRASH CREW MAKE THEIR WAY TO THE **SUGAR HILL RECORDS** COMPOUND, THEY CAN'T HELP BUT TAKE IT ALL IN.

BET!

!!!

STRATEGICALLY, ON THIS DAY, SYLVIA **DECIDES** TO GIVE HER ESTABLISHED ARTISTS SOME **ROYALTIES.**

HEY, I'M MASTER GEE! WHOOPS!

ALL OF THESE **GAMBITS** PAY OFF. THE CRASH CREW'S FIRST SINGLE WITH SUGARHILL IS "**WE WANT TO ROCK.**"

TRY TO BE HAPPY, JUST LIKE THE **CRASH CREW!**

THE FURIOUS FIVE HAVE A BEEF WITH THE CRASH OVER THE USE OF THE "**FREEDOM**" BREAK, WHICH IS THE BACKBONE TO POPULAR SONGS BY **BOTH** GROUPS.

DON'T EVEN **THINK** ABOUT **PERFORMIN'** THAT SHIT AROUND US!

RATHER THAN A STANDARD **RAP BATTLE**, THE TWO FACTIONS AGREE TO PLAY A GAME OF **FOOTBALL** TO SETTLE THE SCORE. OTHER **SUGAR HILL** ACTS EVEN OUT THE REST OF THE **PLAYERS.** THE FURIOUS FIVE GET **BIG BANK HANK** ON THEIR TEAM.

NEEDLESS TO SAY, THE CRASH CREW **DOESN'T** GET TO PLAY "**HIGH POWERED RAP**" WHEN ON TOUR WITH GRANDMASTER FLASH AND THE FURIOUS FIVE.

FLASH... ONE TIME!!

CHRIS STEIN AND DEBORAH HARRY, THE LEADERS OF THE BAND BLONDIE, ARE MAJOR PATRONS OF FRED FAB FIVE'S ARTWORK.

WHEN YOU SEE THEM, FIND OUT IF THEY'LL DO MUSIC FOR OUR FILM!

DEBBIE HAS BEEN EXCITED FOR DAYS TO SEE FRED.

THE NEW CANVAS IS GREAT, FREDDY!

WE JUST PUT TOGETHER A NEW PIECE I WANT TO PLAY FOR YOU!

FAB FIVE FREDDY TOLD ME EVERYBODY'S FLY DJ'S SPINNIN' I SAID "MY MY," FLASH IS FAST, FLASH IS COOL...

HAW!

WHAT IS THIS?

LIKE IT, FREDDY?

...AND THEN YOU'RE IN THE MAN FROM MARS, YOU GO OUT AT NIGHT, EATIN' CARS, YOU EAT CADILLACS, LINCOLNS TOO, MERCURIES AND SUBARUS...

HA HAW!

WE CALL IT, "RAPTURE"!

YO, IT'S BETTER THAN HOME COOKIN'!

FRED AND CHARLIE AHEARN HAVE BECOME VERY SERIOUS ABOUT MAKING A HIP HOP MOVIE. THEY CAN'T SEEM TO FIND FUNDING IN THE U.S., BUT THERE ARE SOME INTERESTED PARTIES IN GERMANY, OF ALL PLACES.

I HAVE ONE QUESTION...

...IS GRAFFITI ONLY GOING TO BE ON CANVAS FROM NOW ON?

TAKING A DETOUR THROUGH ITALY TO SEE SOME ART IN MILAN WITH HIS FRIENDS FROM THE TALKING HEADS, CHRIS FRANTZ AND TINA WEYMOUTH, FRED GETS REINTRODUCED TO RAPTURE IN A NEW CONTEXT...

FAB FIVE FREDDY TOLD ME EVERYBODY'S FLY...

WHAT! CHRIS AND DEBBIE'S SONG IS ON THE RADIO!?

I THOUGHT THEY MADE IT UP, FOR ME, AS A JOKE!!

AN EXCERPT FROM GRANDMASTER FLASH AND THE FURIOUS FIVE'S *SUPERRAPPIN'*...

AS SURE AS 3 TIMES 2 IS 6, YA SAY FLASH IS THE KING OF THE... QUICK MIX!!!

IN ACTUALITY...

IT'S ALL PHONY BULLSHIT, SYLVIA!!

I AIN'T ON **NO** RECORDS! SINCE WE STARTED MAKIN' THEM I BEEN **SITTING ON THE SIDELINES!!!**

I'M THE **ILLEST** DJ OUT THERE! **MY NAME RINGS OUT!** EVERY TIME I THROW A JAM THE CLUBS IS PACKED. I AIN'T BEING REPRESENTED RIGHT.

I GOTTA SHOW PEOPLE WHAT I'M ABOUT! **ON WAX! NO HOUSE BAND! NO FURIOUS FIVE! NO BULLSHIT!** JUST ME, MY **RECORDS**, AND MY **SKILLS!!**

OKAY...

BREAKING **MORE** NEW GROUND, SUGARHILL GOES ON TO RELEASE **THE ADVENTURES OF GRANDMASTER FLASH ON THE WHEELS OF STEEL**, A CONTINUOUS, **7-MINUTE** DISPLAY OF FLASH'S **QUICK MIX** THEORY. INSISTING ON DOING IT **LIVE**, WITH **NO** PRODUCTION **SHORTCUTS**, IT TAKES HIM 3 OR 4 TRYS TO GET IT JUST **RIGHT**...

FLASH IS GOOD...

FLASH IS GOOD.

FLASH IS ...GOOD TIMES...

SAMPLES USED TO MAKE THE RECORD

QUEEN: ANOTHER ONE BITES THE DUST
INCREDIBLE BONGO BAND: APACHE
CHIC: GOOD TIMES
BLONDIE: RAPTURE
SUGARHILL GANG: 8TH WONDER
SPOONIE GEE: MONSTER JAM
GRANDMASTER FLASH AND THE FURIOUS FIVE: FREEDOM
GRANDMASTER FLASH AND THE FURIOUS FIVE: BIRTHDAY PARTY
SUGARHILL GANG: RAPPER'S DELIGHT
THE HELLERS: LIFE STORY

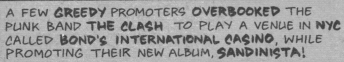

A FEW **GREEDY** PROMOTERS **OVERBOOKED** THE PUNK BAND **THE CLASH** TO PLAY A VENUE IN **NYC** CALLED **BOND'S INTERNATIONAL CASINO**, WHILE PROMOTING THEIR NEW ALBUM, **SANDINISTA!**

THIS PLACE HOLDS NO MORE THAN **3500**... MAXIMUM!!

THE BAND **VOWS** TO HONOR **EVERY** TICKET.

>FEH<

WE'LL JUST HAVE TO PLAY A FEW MORE GIGS.

WITH **ELEVEN** NEW SHOWS TO PLAY, THE CLASH SCRAMBLES FOR NEW **OPENING ACTS.**

SO FAR YOU HEARD MY VOICE, BUT I BROUGHT TWO FRIENDS ALONG...

...SO, NEXT ON THE MIC IS MY MAN, **HANK**, SO C'MON HANK SING THIS SONG.

SPECIAL K...

SUNSHINE

KOOL MOE DEE...

ON TIME!

GRANDMASTER FLASH AND THE **FURIOUS FIVE** ARE SCHEDULED TO OPEN **TWO** DAYS IN A ROW.

YOU SODS DON'T GET IT? THESE MEN INSPIRED... THE MAGNIFICENT SEVEN!

1, 2, 3, 4!

FUCK DISCO!

THE FOLLOWING NIGHT...

WE'RE GONNA MAKE FIVE EMCEES SOUND LIKE ONE!

80

GIVING IT **ONE** MORE SHOT, **AFRIKA BAMBAATAA** AGREES TO MAKE A RECORD FOR TOM SILVERMAN'S NEW LABEL, **TOMMYBOY.**

THE **JAZZY FIVE** BE NEXT IN LINE...

ARTHUR BAKER, A DJ, PRODUCER, AND REVIEWER FOR SILVERMAN'S **DANCE MUSIC REPORT,** IS THE **ONLY** GUY THAT TOM KNOWS WHO CAN HELP MAKE THE **RECORD.**

WE'RE THINKIN' OF MAKIN' A RECORD BASED ON A NEW **HIT** SONG.

WE'RE THINKING OF **USING** EITHER **GENIUS OF LOVE** ✳, OR **FUNKY SENSATION!**

✳ BY **TOM TOM CLUB,** CHRIS FRANTZ AND TINA WEYMOUTH. FRIENDS WITH **FAB FIVE FREDDY**

GWEN McCRAE IS BUTTER!

THEIR COLLABORATION GOES ON TO SELL **35,000** COPIES. SILVERMAN IS HAPPY WITH THIS EARLY EFFORT, BUT HE'S NOT EXACTLY RACING TO PUT THE **JAZZY 5** BACK ON VINYL.

BAM, WE WANT TO MAKE **ANOTHER** RECORD. WHO ELSE DO YOU HAVE IN MIND?

THE SOUL SONIC FORCE, **BUT...**

...I DON'T JUST WANNA KEEP MAKIN' RAP VERSIONS OF REKKIDS THAT ARE HITS ALREADY. I WANNA DO SOMETHIN' MORE **FUNKIER!**

LIKE WHAT?

I BEEN LISTENING TO SOME **BAD** GERMAN WHITE BOYS LATELY. THIS **TRANS - EUROPE EXPRESS** IS SWEETER THAN BEAR MEAT!

KRAFTWERK!? I LOVE KRAFTWERK!

BEING A **DIVERSE** FAN OF MUSIC, YOUNG **RICK RUBIN'S** WHIMSY POINTS HIM IN THE DIRECTION TO START HIS **OWN** BAND, **THE PRICKS**. EVEN THOUGH HE GETS THE **BEST** EQUIPMENT MONEY CAN BUY...

UGH! I JUST CAN'T GET WHAT I HAVE IN MY HEAD TO **TRANSLATE**...

DON'T WORRY, **RICK**. YOU DO A LOT WITH A LITTLE.

IN SPITE OF THEIR **INEPTITUDE**, AND THANKS TO THE RIGOROUS TOURING SCHEDULE OF THE **USUAL** HEADLINERS, THE PRICKS GET A CHANCE TO PLAY **C.B.G.B.'S**.

FUCK ALLA YOUZ GUYS!

YOU MOOKS AREN'T WORTH OUR MUSIC! **FUCK OFF!**

ARTISTIC LICENSE

RAMONES

POLICE!

SHOW'S OVER, NOW, FELLA.

FL
YO

15 MINUTES LATER...

DUDE, YOU SHOULDA TOLD ME YOU WERE GONNA DECK ME WITH A **GUITAR**.

TOOK IT LIKE A **CHAMP**, MAN!

LOVES PRO WRESTLING

RICK'S DAD IS AN AUX. POLICEMAN FOR NASSAU COUNTY.

ON A RITUALISTIC, WEEKLY BASIS...

NOTHING? STILL?!

FILMS ON THE BORDER

VOICE

Revolt in Reaga

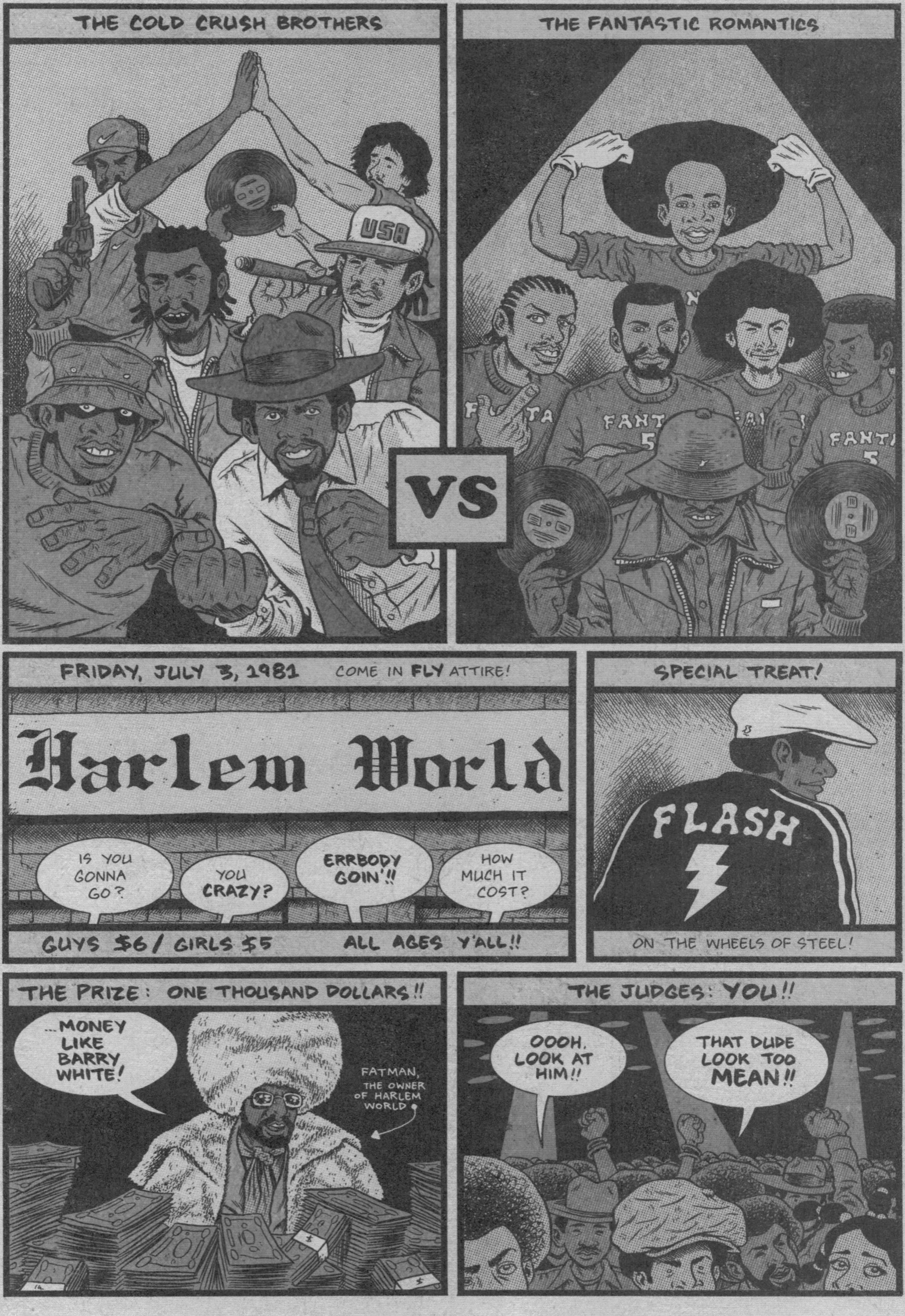
THE COLD CRUSH BROTHERS
THE FANTASTIC ROMANTICS
USA
VS
FANTA
FRIDAY, JULY 3, 1981
COME IN FLY ATTIRE!
Harlem World
IS YOU GONNA GO?
YOU CRAZY?
ERRBODY GOIN'!!
HOW MUCH IT COST?
GUYS $6 / GIRLS $5
ALL AGES Y'ALL!!
SPECIAL TREAT!
FLASH
ON THE WHEELS OF STEEL!
THE PRIZE: ONE THOUSAND DOLLARS!!
...MONEY LIKE BARRY WHITE!
FATMAN, THE OWNER OF HARLEM WORLD
THE JUDGES: YOU!!
OOOH, LOOK AT HIM!!
THAT DUDE LOOK TOO MEAN!!

THIS **POLARIZING** BATTLE HAS BEEN INEVITABLE. IN THE BRONX TAKING SIDES IS ALMOST A **POLITICAL** OR **SPIRITUAL** DECISION.

YOU'RE CRAZY!

LEADING UP TO THE JAM, IF MEMBERS OF THE **COLD CRUSH** AND THE **FANTASTIC** CROSSED PATHS IN THE STREETS...

WE GONNA WIPE THE FLOOR WITCH Y'ALL!

!!

BUT, **REALLY**...

THINK THEY BOUGHT THE DRAMA?

HIT THIS!

THE EARLY **HYPE** DOES ITS JOB!

I HEARD CAZ KEEPS GUNS...

GONNA BE A SERIOUS THROWDOWN!

POLICE IS WATCHIN'!!

THE COLD CRUSH BROTHERS PULL OUT ALL STOPS BY DAZZLING THE CROWD WITH **FRESH** THEATRICS AND BRAND NEW, **UNTESTED** ROUTINES.

OTHER EMCEES CAN'T DEAL WITH US, BECAUSE WE ARE THE FOUR KNOWN AS THE **COLD CRUSH**!

THE FANTASTIC ROMANTICS **EXCEL** AT WHAT THEY DO **BEST**.

DOT-A-ROCK, ARE YOU READY TO WIN THE G?

THE GUSTO IS GOIN' HOME WITH ME! YO, **MASTER ROB** ARE YOU READY TO WIN THE G?

THE GUSTO IS COMIN' HOME WITH ME! SO **WHIPPER WHIP** ARE YOU READY TO WIN THE G?

T IS W

THE $1000, THE CROWD DE-CIDES, GOES TO...

FANTASTIC!!

COLD CRUSH!!

COLD CRUSH!

THE COLD CRUSH BROS HAVE THOUGHTS ABOUT THE OUTCOME...

YO! THEY BROUGHT THEY OWN **FANS**! WE DIDN'T BRING NO ONE!

THEM **JUDGES** JUS' HEARD THE GIRLS IN THE **FRONT**.

VERY RAPIDLY, **BOOTLEGS** OF THE **BATTLE** MAKE THEIR WAY TO **ALL** 5 BOROUGHS, INCLUDING SPECIFICALLY **HOLLIS**, QUEENS.

IT WAS HOW MUCH, D?

$9. SAVED UP LUNCH MONEY TO GET IT.

JASON MIZELL

BATTLES AND COMPETITIONS SEEM TO BE HARLEM WORLD'S MAIN SHOWCASE THESE DAYS. THE JAMS ARE MOSTLY PROMOTED BY KOOL DJ AJ AND USUALLY WON BY BUSY BEE STARSKI.

IT AIN'T GONNA BE NO DIFFERENT THIS TIME, NEITHER!

HEY!

WATCH IT, FOO!

I'M KNOCKIN' OUT ALL BUMS!

I'M TAKIN' OUT ALL THE CHUMPS!

AWW... THERE HE GO!

HA HA!

SOMEONE TAKE A PITCHER OF ME WIT' DIS! IT'S MINES!!

I BE BACK TA CLAIM IT IN 'BOUT HA'F AN HOUR!

EXIT

AW YEAH? YOU CAN'T BEAT MOE DEE!

OOH SHIT!

PSSSST!

IT'S ON NOW!

?

MAN, I DON'T CARE WHO THEY IS!

ANYBODY TRIES TO STEP TO ME ITS GONNA BE SUICIDE!

RESTROOMS

YOU CRAZY! MOE DEE'LL SMOKE YOU!

LIKE I SAID! SUICIDE!

OOH, BUSY BEE SET IT OFF!

SHIT IS CRAZ

AS IS CUSTOM, BUSY BEE GETS TO BE THE FINAL, HEADLINING PARTICIPANT IN THE COMPETITION. PULLING FROM HIS YEARS AND YEARS OF EXPERIENCE IN ROCKIN' THE HOUSE...

IS MANHATTAN IN THE HOUSE!

NO!

NAW!

IS THE BRONX IN THE HOUSE!

NO!

YAY!

WOO!

FUCK!

YEAH

!!!!

HO!

YO, BUS' IT, BIZ!

GO OFF!

BRONX!

WO!

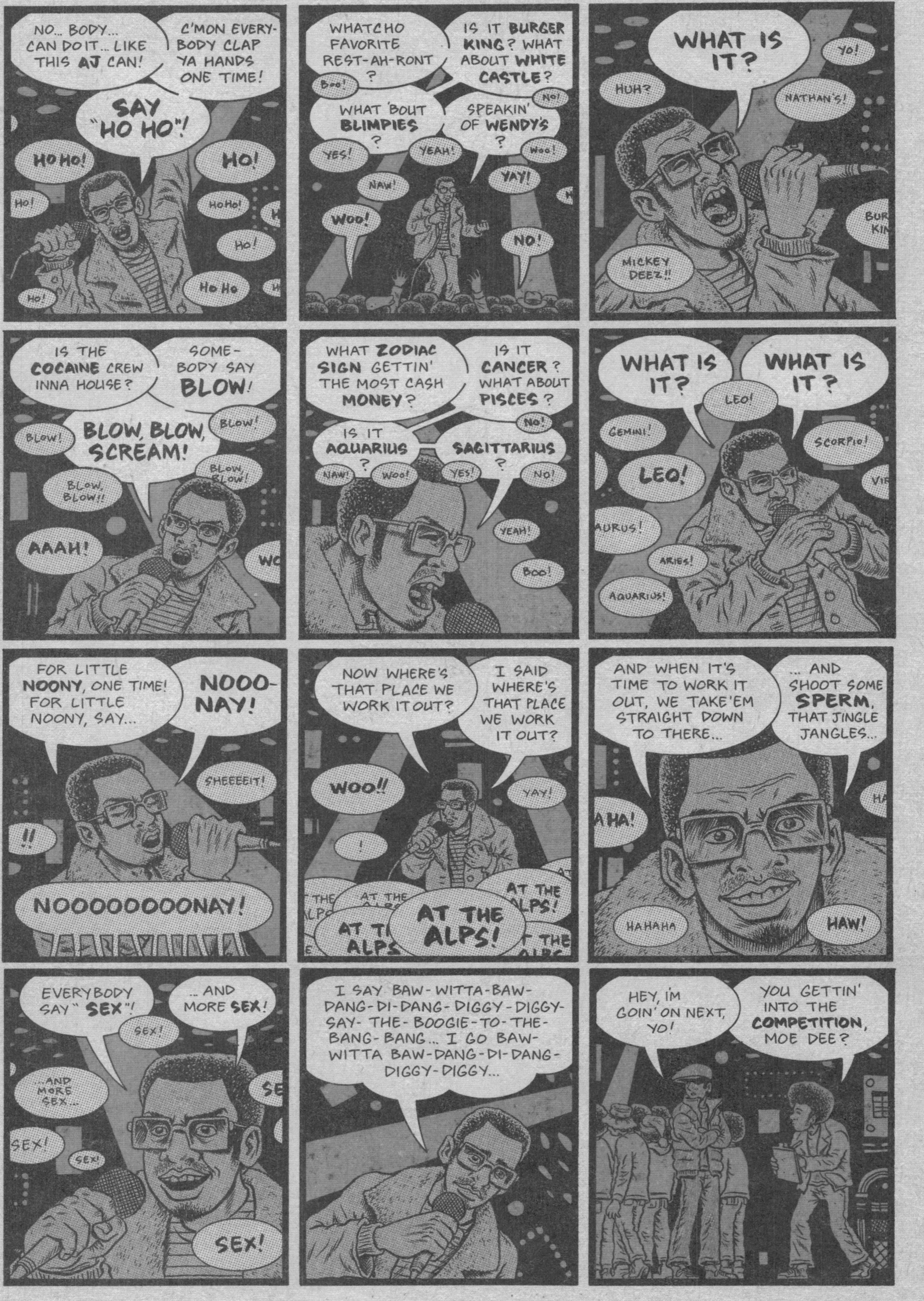
NO... BODY... CAN DO IT... LIKE THIS AJ CAN!
C'MON EVERYBODY CLAP YA HANDS ONE TIME!
SAY "HO HO"!
HO HO!
HO!
HO!
HoHo!
Ho!
Ho Ho
Ho!
WHATCHO FAVORITE REST-AH-RONT?
IS IT BURGER KING? WHAT ABOUT WHITE CASTLE?
Boo!
WHAT 'BOUT BLIMPIES?
SPEAKIN' OF WENDY'S?
NO!
YES!
YEAH!
WOO!
NAW!
YAY!
WOO!
NO!
WHAT IS IT?
YO!
HUH?
NATHAN'S!
MICKEY DEEZ!!
IS THE COCAINE CREW INNA HOUSE?
SOMEBODY SAY BLOW!
BLOW, BLOW, SCREAM!
BLOW!
BLOW!
BLOW, BLOW!!
BLOW, BLOW!
AAAH!
WHAT ZODIAC SIGN GETTIN' THE MOST CASH MONEY?
IS IT CANCER? WHAT ABOUT PISCES?
NO!
IS IT AQUARIUS?
SAGITTARIUS?
NAW!
WOO!
YES!
NO!
YEAH!
BOO!
WHAT IS IT?
WHAT IS IT?
LEO!
GEMINI!
SCORPIO!
LEO!
ARIES!
AQUARIUS!
FOR LITTLE NOONY, ONE TIME! FOR LITTLE NOONY, SAY...
NOOO-NAY!
SHEEEEIT!
!!
NOOOOOOOOONAY!
NOW WHERE'S THAT PLACE WE WORK IT OUT?
I SAID WHERE'S THAT PLACE WE WORK IT OUT?
WOO!!
YAY!
!
AT THE ALPS!
AT THE ALPS!
AND WHEN IT'S TIME TO WORK IT OUT, WE TAKE 'EM STRAIGHT DOWN TO THERE...
... AND SHOOT SOME SPERM, THAT JINGLE JANGLES...
HAHAHA
HAW!
EVERYBODY SAY "SEX"!
... AND MORE SEX!
SEX!
...AND MORE SEX...
SEX!
SEX!
SEX!
I SAY BAW-WITTA-BAW-DANG-DI-DANG-DIGGY-DIGGY-SAY-THE-BOOGIE-TO-THE-BANG-BANG... I GO BAW-WITTA BAW-DANG-DI-DANG-DIGGY-DIGGY...
HEY, I'M GOIN' ON NEXT, YO!
YOU GETTIN' INTO THE COMPETITION, MOE DEE?

ONCE AGAIN, MC **BUSY BEE** WITH **KOOL DJ AJ.** COMING UP NEXT FROM **THE TREACHEROUS THREE** EMCEES, **KOOL MOE DEE.**

HEY BABY, YOU TRYNA COME DOWN- STAIRS AN' SMOKE THIS? I GOT THE BUBBLYS TOO.

SURE, BIZ!

EXIT

...AN' I'M GOIN' WIF 'IM!

1,2,1,2, **PARTY PEOPLE** IN THE PLACE TO BE! MY NAME IS MC **KOOL MOE DEE** OF THE TREACHEROUS **THREE**! MY MAN **L.A. SUNSHINE** IN THE PLACE TO BE!

WE GONNA SET SOMETHING STRAIGHT IN THE PLACE TO BE...

MY MAN, **BUSY BEE STARSKI** ...

HOW MANY PEOPLE THINK **BUSY BEE** ROCK THE HOUSE?

I'M ON HIS DICK!

YEP!

UM HUH

AAAH!

NO!

SURE...

YEAH!

YO!

UH HUH

AH!

WOO!

WORD!

I HEARD THAT, BUT, IF YOU NOTICE IT OR NOT I HEARD A LOT OF **SHIT**! BUSY BEE'S POPPIN' SHIT SAYIN' HE'LL **TAKE OUT** ANY EMCEE AN' ALL THAT!

I GIVE IT TO THE MAN, HE CAN ROCK THE **CROWD**, BUT WHEN IT COMES TO WRITING RHYMES, NO WAY HE CAN FUCK **AROUND**, AND I'M A PROVE DAT RIGHT **NOW**!

REMEMBER THIS! **DJ LEE** YOU GOT IT TOGETHER YET? ONE. TWO... **ONE FOR THE TREBLE, TWO FOR THE BASS,** C'MON EASY LEE* AND LET'S ROCK THIS PLACE!!

* DJ EASY LEE SPINS THE BREAKS FOR THE TREACHEROUS THREE.

NOW, **BUSY BEE** I DON'T MEAN TO **BE BOLD,** BUT PUT THAT "BAW WITTA-BAW" BULLSHIT ON **HOLD.** WE GONNA **GIT** RIGHT DOWN TO THE **NITTY-GRIT,** GONNA TELL A LITTLE STORY WHY YOU AIN'T **SHIT**!

THERE AIN'T AN EMCEE'S COCK THAT YOU DON'T **HUG**. YOU EVEN BIT YO' NAME FROM THE **LOVEBUG**. TO BITE A NIGGA'S NAME, THAT'S SOME LOW DOWN **SHIT**, IF YOU WAS MONEY, MAN, YOU'D BE **COUNTERFEIT**!

I GOTTA GIVE IT TO YOU, THOUGH YOU CAN **ROCK**, BUT, EVERYBODY KNOWS YOU'RE ON THE **FURIOUS JOCK**... AND I REMEMBER BUSY FROM THE OLDEN **TIMES**, WHEN MY MAN, **SPOONIE GEE**, USED TO SELL YOU **RHYMES**!

REMEMBER THAT RHYME CALLED "DITTY-BAW-**DITTY**"? MAN, GODDAMN THAT **SHIT** WAS A **PITY**. TOO **HOT** TO **TROT**, I'M HIP TO **ROCK** THE **SPOT**. SPOONIE GEE ROCK IT WHETHER YA LIKE IT OR **NOT**!

HE PAID FOR THE RHYMES, ASKED FOR 'EM **TWICE**. HE SAID "SPOONIE GEE, I'D BUY AT ANY **PRICE**." WHEN SPOONIE FINALLY SOLD 'EM, OH WHAT A **RELIEF**, BUSY BEE STOLE IT LIKE A FUCKIN' **THIEF**!

"EVERY TIME I HEAR **IT**, I THROW A **FIT**, PARTY AFTER PARTY, THE SAME OL' **SHIT**. REKKID AFTER REKKID, **RHYME** AFTER **RHYME**, ALWAYS WANT TO KNOW THEIR **ZODIAC** SIGN..."

PSSSSST!

?

HE CHANGED THE SHIT TO "YOUR FAVORITE **JEANS**," C'MON BUSY BEE TELL ME WHAT THAT **MEANS**? UH, BRUTHA-MAN DON'T YOU SAY **NUTTIN'**, I'M NOT FINISHED YET I GOTTA TELL YOU **SUMPTHIN'**!

"TOO **HOT** TO **TROT**, I'M HIP TO ROCK THE **SPOT**. I'M GONNA ROCK YA ASS WHETHER YOU LIKE IT OR **NOT**. I'LL TAKE THE TITLE RIGHT ON THE **SPOT**... HOW CAN I TAKE A TITLE YOU AIN'T **GOT**?"

!!!

YOU'RE NOT NUMBAH ONE, YOU'RE NOT EVEN THE **BEST** AND YOU CAN'T WIN NO REAL EMCEE **CONTEST**!

SHUT UP!

"...CELEBRITY CLUBS, THOSE ARE THE KINDS YOU CAN **WIN**, THEY ARE ALL SET UP BEFORE WE COME **IN**, BUT IN A BATTLE LIKE THIS YOU KNOW YOU'LL **LOSE**. BETWEEN ME AND **YOU**, WHO DO **YOU** THINK THEY'LL **CHOOSE**?"

WELL, IF **YOU** THINK IT'S **YOU**, I GOT BAD **NEWS**, BECAUSE TO HEAR YOUR NAME, YOU'RE GONNA HEAR SOME "**BOOS**." 'CAUSE YOU'RE FAKIN' THE FUNK. 'CAUSE YOU'RE FAKIN' THE FUNK...

"... AND AT THE END OF THIS RHYME YOU CAN CALL ME "**UNK-OL'** MOE DEE"! CALL ME **UNCLE**! ROCK THE HOUSE **Y'ALL**!

I'M ON MOE DEE DICK!

...BUT YOU WANNA **BE**! BIZ, YOU **WANNABE**! AND YOU KNOW YOU WANNA BE ANOTHER KOOL MOE DEE. SO LET'S ALL **CHANT** BECAUSE YOU KNOW YOU **CAN'T**, AND EVERYBODY SALUTE THE NEW EMCEE **CHAMP**...

... NOW THAT "BAW-DITTY-BAW-DANG-DI-DANG-**DANG**" SOUNDS PRETTY GOOD, BUT, IT AIN'T NO **THANG**...

I'M THE **SUPER SCOOPER**, PARTY **POOPER**, MAN WITH ALL THE **SUPER DUPER** DISCO **BREAKS**, A MAN WHO NEVER MAKES **MISTAKES**... A RAPPIN' **LORD**, I'M NOT A **BORE**... THE BADDEST MAN YOU EVER **SAW**. THE MONEY-**MAKIN'**, EARTH-**QUAKIN'** MAN WHO GETS THE PARTY **SHAKIN'**!

WHOA!

WOW!

MURDER!

AND SO, **MOE DEE** CONTINUES OBLITERATING **BUSY BEE** FOR TWO MORE MINUTES OF **MAYHEM**. THE **BATTLE** IS RECORDED AND THE **BOOTLEG** GETS DISTRIBUTED **VIRALLY**, THUS CREATING THE TEMPLATE FOR MICROPHONE CHALLENGES THIS POINT FORWARD!

FUCK! MR. MAGIC IS PLAYING IT, TOO?

...CHILL ON OUT...

IF YOUR SONG IS **NUMBER ONE** ON **BILLBOARD**, OPPORTUNITIES ABOUND!

FREDDY! THANKS TO **RAPTURE**, I'M GONNA GET TO HOST **SATURDAY NIGHT LIVE!!**

NO JIVE?

PART OF THE GIG IS TO PICK THE **MUSICAL** PERFORMANCE!

I WANT A **STREET RAP** GROUP TO PLAY THAT NIGHT.

AW POOP! I BLINKED!!

HMMM... WAY I SEE IT, YOU GOT TWO SOLID OPTIONS. **GRANDMASTER FLASH AND THE FURIOUS FIVE** GOT MAJOR CLOUT ON THE STREETS...

MY OWN **PERSONAL** FAVORITES, THOUGH, ARE THE **FUNKY FOUR PLUS ONE.**

OOH! THE FUNKY FOUR HAVE A GIRL IN THE GROUP, JUST LIKE **BLONDIE.** THINK THEY'LL DO IT?

I'LL TALK TO SYLVIA. ME AND CHARLIE HAVE SOME BUSINESS TO DISCUSS WITH HER ANYHOW.

DAMMIT!

AT THE **SUGAR HILL** COMPOUND, **CHARLIE AHEARN** AND **FAB FIVE FREDDY** CAN'T MAKE MUCH HEADWAY GETTING THE LABEL'S PERMISSION TO MAKE A FILM WITH THE FUNKY FOUR PLUS ONE.

MISS SYLVIA. WHAT IF WE SAID WE COULD GET THEM TO PERFORM ON SATURDAY NIGHT LIVE?

THEN CAN THEY BE IN OUR PICTURE?

THINKING ABOUT IT, I WOULD **LOVE** TO GET THE **SUGARHILL GANG** ON THAT SHOW.

WELL, LET US PULL A FEW STRINGS AN' SEE WHAT HAPPENS.

ON THE **FEBRUARY 14, 1981,** EPISODE OF **SATURDAY NIGHT LIVE,** DEBORAH HARRY INTRODUCES THE NATION TO THE **FIRST** RAPPERS TO APPEAR ON THE PROGRAM, **MINUTES** BEFORE THE CREDITS ROLL...

WELL WE JUST CAN'T MISS WITH A BEAT LIKE THIS...

THE FUNKY FOUR ALSO BRING OUT **DJ BREAKOUT** FRONT AND CENTER, EVEN THOUGH HOUSE BANDS CREATE ALL THE **MUSIC** FOR THEIR RECORDS.

...THAT'S THE JOINT!

YOU GUYS ARE THE **BEST!** I WANT YOU ALL TO COME ON TOUR WITH **BLONDIE!**

FUH SHO!

YEAH!

WORD!

THINKIN' ABOUT IT, WE'LL PROB'LY HAVE TO CHECK WITH MS. SYLVIA TO SEE IF IT'S COOL.

I'D BE HAPPY TO HAVE OUR LAWYERS CHECK OUT YOUR CONTRACTS, IF YOU WANT?

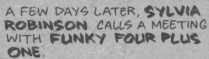
A FEW DAYS LATER, **SYLVIA ROBINSON** CALLS A MEETING WITH **FUNKY FOUR PLUS ONE.**

NAW, Y'ALL DON'T NEED TO GO ON TOUR WITH BLONDIE. Y'ALL DON'T NEED TO BE IN ANY FILM, EITHER. I HAVE OTHER PLANS FOR YOU.

BY THE WAY, DID THOSE **LAWYERS** EXPLAIN THAT I SIGNED EACH OF YOU **INDEPENDENTLY,** AND THAT **SUGAR HILL** OWNS THE FUNKY FOUR PLUS ONE?

THAT MEANS THAT ANY OF YOU CAN BE **FIRED** FROM THE GROUP AND **REPLACED.** SO ARE Y'ALL WITH **SUGAR HILL** OR NOT?

WE'RE WITH YOU, MISS ROB.

UH HUH...

FOR SOME, THE "**BUSINESS**" OF HIP HOP HAS TAKEN ALL THE **FUN** OUT OF THE CULTURE.

I DON'T KNOW, RODNEY. I MIGHT HAVE TO BREAK AWAY FROM THE GROUP.

I'M WITCHU, MAN. AIN'T NUTTIN' TO IT BUT TO DO IT!

AFTER **K.K. ROCKWELL** AND **RODNEY C** FORMALLY LEAVE THE **FUNKY FOUR,** THEIR FIRST PHONE CALL IS TO **CHARLIE AHEARN,** WHO'S STILL BUSY SECURING **FUNDING** FOR THE HIP HOP MOVIE HE WANTS TO MAKE.

DON'T WORRY. I PROMISE YOU BOYS WILL **DEFINITELY** HAVE A PLACE IN MY **FILM.**

WITH THE **NEW**, RISING POPULARITY OF **HOME VIDEO**, BLONDIE HAS SIGNED A DEAL TO CREATE A TAPE FULL OF **MUSIC VIDEOS**. RIGHT NOW, THOUGH, THE PRODUCTION ON THE SET OF **RAPTURE** IS AT A STANDSTILL.

BUT, WHERE THE HECK IS **HE**?

DON'T SWEAT IT. I KNOW WHO CAN TAKE HIS PLACE.

SINCE **GRANDMASTER FLASH** IS NO WHERE TO BE FOUND, FILMING RESUMES WITH **JEAN-MICHEL BASQUIAT** FILLING THE ROLE OF **DJ** IN THE VID.

DJ SPINNIN' I SAID "MY MY."

LEE QUINONES AND **FAB FIVE FREDDY** ALSO MAKE THEIR APPEARANCE, IN THE BACKGROUND, DOING WHAT THEY DO BEST.

ON **AUGUST 1, 1981**, A REVOLUTIONARY NEW **CABLE TELEVISION** CHANNEL BEGINS **BROADCASTING** AND IS IN NEED OF A STEADY ROTATION OF CONTENT.

TUCKED BETWEEN **REO SPEEDWAGON'S** "TOUGH GUYS" AND **THE WHO'S** "DON'T LET GO THE COAT," **BLONDIE'S** "RAPTURE" IS THE **48**TH MUSIC VIDEO TO PLAY ON **MTV** THAT FIRST DAY.

CHARLIE AHEARN HAS FINALLY RUSTLED UP A SUITABLE AMOUNT OF **MONEY** TO BEGIN SHOOTING HIS NEXT MOVIE, BUT...

NOW THAT WE CAN'T FILM THE **FUNKY FOUR PLUS ONE**, WHAT DO WE DO?

DON'T EVEN WORRY ABOUT IT, MAN. THERE'S A **COLD CRUSH** JAM LATER. WE'LL THINK ON IT!

UP TO THIS POINT, CHARLIE HAS **NOT** BEEN MUCH OF A FIXTURE ON THE **HIP HOP** SCENE.

YO, PUT THE WEED OUT!

5-O!

EVEN THOUGH HE'S AS **HIGH** AS ANYBODY ELSE IN THE VENUE, **BUSY BEE STARSKI** IS STILL COMPELLED TO SEE WHAT A **WHITE GUY**, TWICE EVERYONE'S AGE, IS DOING IN THE CLUB.

WHY YOU HERE, MAN?

JUST DOING SOME RESEARCH. I'M GONNA BE MAKING A FILM ABOUT HIP HOP.

FOLLOW ME!!

HEY, Y'ALL! I WANTCHOO TO MEET **MY** MOVIE PRODUCER, **CHARLIE AHEARN**.

WE'RE MAKIN' A FLICK ABOUT THIS HERE **HIP HOP** GAME!

DURING SPRING **1981**, RAP MUSIC IS BECOMING POPULAR ENOUGH THAT IT'S HARD FOR **MAINSTREAM** MEDIA TO IGNORE IT.

THE NEW SOUND OF THE 90S! SUDDENLY YOU HEAR IT EVERY-WHERE...

RAP MUSIC! IT'S ALL BEAT, AND ALL TALK!

RAPPIN' TO THE BEAT

YOU CAN'T GET MUCH MORE MAINSTREAM, OR **WHITE**, THAN **HUGH DOWNS**, **STEVE FOX**, AND THE TELEVISION PROGRAM **20/20**.

THERE HAVE BEEN **TALKING BLUES**, AND THINGS LIKE **CONCERTOS** FOR DRUMS, BUT RIGHT **NOW**...

...ALL AROUND US, AND SO **COMPELLING** YOU NEVER MISS THE FACT THAT THERE'S **NO MELODY**...

THEIR 10-MINUTE FEATURE IS GENERALLY POSITIVE TOWARD THIS EMERGING, ALIEN CULTURE. IT SEEMS FITTING THAT THE **FIRST** RAPPERS WE SEE ON THE PROGRAM ARE THE **SUGARHILL GANG** FROM THE RECENT PERFORMANCE ON THE MAY, 30TH EPISODE OF **SOUL TRAIN**.

20/20 CORRESPONDENT **STEVE FOX** GIVES LOTS OF CREDIT TO BLONDIE'S **RAPTURE** FOR INTRODUCING THE CONCEPT TO THE MASSES.

WHAT RAP MUSIC DOES IS IT, LIKE, **REMOVES** THE MIDDLE MAN, BECAUSE IT COULD BE ANYBODY DOING IT...

...IT'S LIKE **DIRECT COMMUNICATION**, AND THAT'S WHAT, LIKE, MUSIC IS!

EXPLAINING THE MODERN, **BRONX** ORIGINS OF **HIP HOP**, THE SHOW HIGHLIGHTS A PUBLIC PARK JAM WITH **KURTIS BLOW** PERFORMING **THE BREAKS**, WHILE **DAVY DMX** IS ON THE TURN-TABLES. AT THIS POINT, THE BREAKS HAS SOLD **680,000** COPIES AND HIT **NUMBER ONE** ON R&B CHARTS.

THESE...   ...ARE...   ...THE...

BREAKS!

THE PIECE ALSO DOES A GOOD JOB RELATING THE DEEPER ORIGINS OF THE CULTURE TO LONG-STANDING TRADITIONS IN THE BLACK SOUTH, LIKE THE **CALL AND RESPONSE** ELEMENTS OF CHURCH SERMONS, RHYME TALK IN GAMES, AND OLD STORY RHYMES.

HEY CONCENTRATION, WHERE HAVE YOU **BEEN**? 'ROUND THE CORNER AND BACK **AGAIN**. STOLE MY **MONEY** AND MY **HONEY**. PAPA GOT THE HICCUPS, MAMA GOT THE **SLICE**...

SOME OF RAPPING'S **FOREFATHERS** ARE SPECIFICALLY MENTIONED IN THE SEGMENT.

CAB CALLOWAY	JAMES BROWN	MUHAMMAD ALI	H. RAP BROWN

ALI SWINGS WIF A LEF', ALI SWINGS WIF A **RIGHT**. LOOK AT THE KID CARRY THE **FIGHT!**

'CAUSE IF AMERICA DON'T COME 'ROUND... AMERICA SHOULD BE BREAKED DOWN!

JOCKO HENDERSON, A 1960S DJ, IS INTERVIEWED DEMONSTRATING SOME OF HIS OLD PATTER THAT MADE HIM **FAMOUS** ON PHILADELPHIA **RADIO**.

EEE-TIDDLY-**OCK**, **HO!** THIS IS THE **JOCK**, AND I'M BACK ON THE **SCENE** WITH THE RECORD **MACHINE**...

SAYIN' **GOO**-BOP-A-**DOO**, HOW DO YOU **DO**?

SNAP! SNAP! SNAP!

ONE CONCEIT OF THE SHOW DISPLAYS HOW RAP CAN BE USED IN OTHER FACETS OF LIFE, LIKE PROMOTING VOTING, FOR EXAMPLE. JOCKO CREATED AN EDUCATIONAL PROGRAM WHICH USES RAP.

THE DECLARATION OF INDEPENDENCE IS THE FIGHT TO STAND ON YOUR **OWN**...

THE COUNTRY WANTS TO WALK INSTEAD OF CRAWL AND MAKE DECISIONS... ALL **ALONE**...

SNAP! SNAP! SNAP!

OF COURSE, MANY REGARD THIS NEW RAP PHENOMENON AS A **FAD** AND THIS IS ALSO REFLECTED WITHIN THESE 10 MINUTES.

I LIVE UP ON THE UPPER EAST SIDE IN A TOWNHOUSE WITH A **STAFF**. I'VE GOT A LIVE-IN **MAID**, A BUTLER, AND **VALET** WHO LAYS OUT MY CLOTHES AND DRAWS A **BATH**.

OVERALL, **STEVE FOX** DOES A PRETTY DECENT AND **FAIR** JOB EXPOSING RAP CULTURE TO THE WORLD. IN THE END, THOUGH, HE **ALSO** DOES A PRETTY GREAT JOB LETTING **HIP HOPPERS** KNOW WHAT THE MAINSTREAM THINKS OF THE MUSIC.

NOT EVERYONE CAN SING...

...BUT ANYONE CAN **RAP!**

NEXT ▷ IT'S LIKE A JUNGLE SOMETIMES ON THE **PLANET ROCK!!**

PINUPS

- BEASTIE BOYS BY JEFFREY BROWN
- AFRIKA BAMBAATAA BY JIM MAHFOOD
- FAT BOYS BY TOM SCIOLI
- GRANDMASTER FLASH AND THE FURIOUS FIVE BY BEN MARRA
- VANILLA ICE BY JIM RUGG
- RUN DMC BY DAN ZETTWOCH
- ERIC B. AND RAKIM BY JOHN PORCELLINO
- SALT N PEPA BY NATE POWELL
- KRS ONE BY BRANDON GRAHAM
- SNOOP DOGG BY FAREL DALRYMPLE

MIN-ONE SAYS:

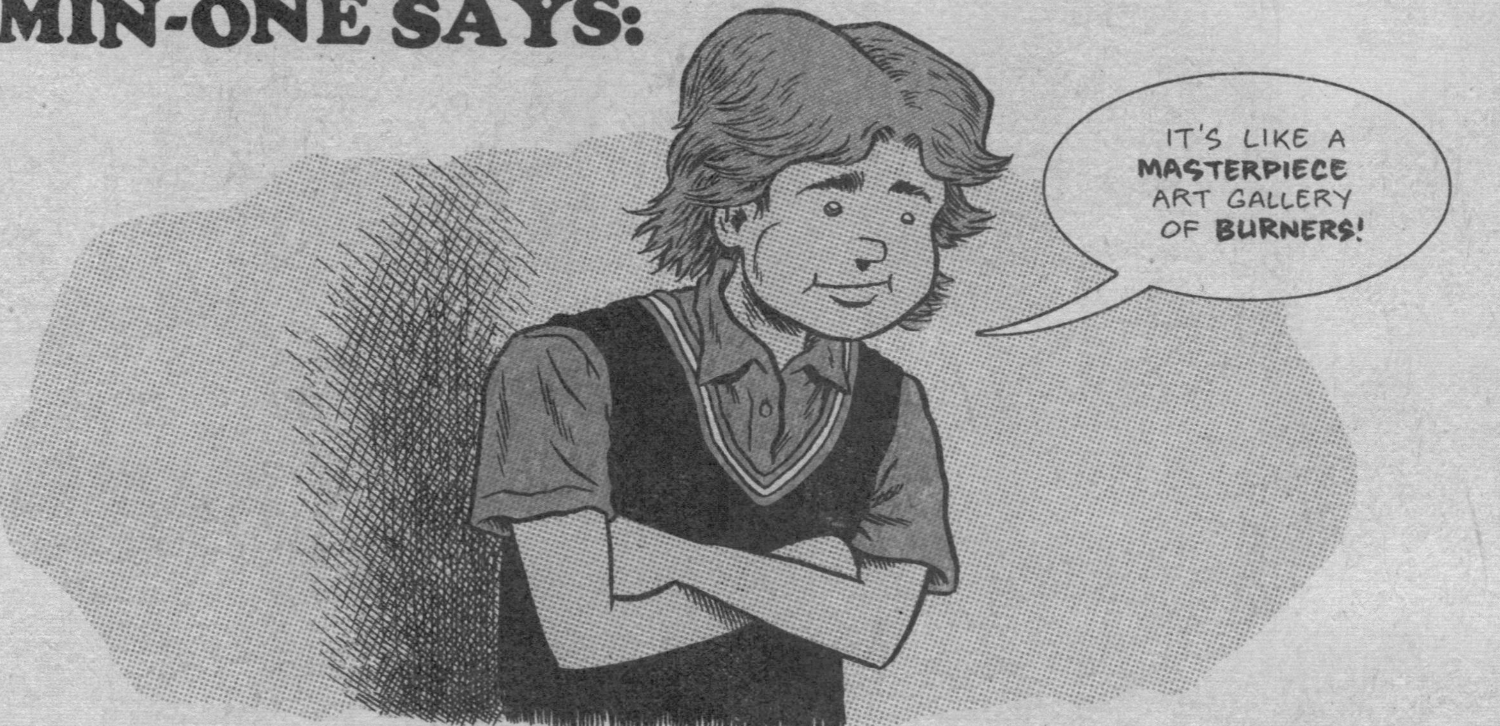
IT'S LIKE A **MASTERPIECE** ART GALLERY OF **BURNERS**!

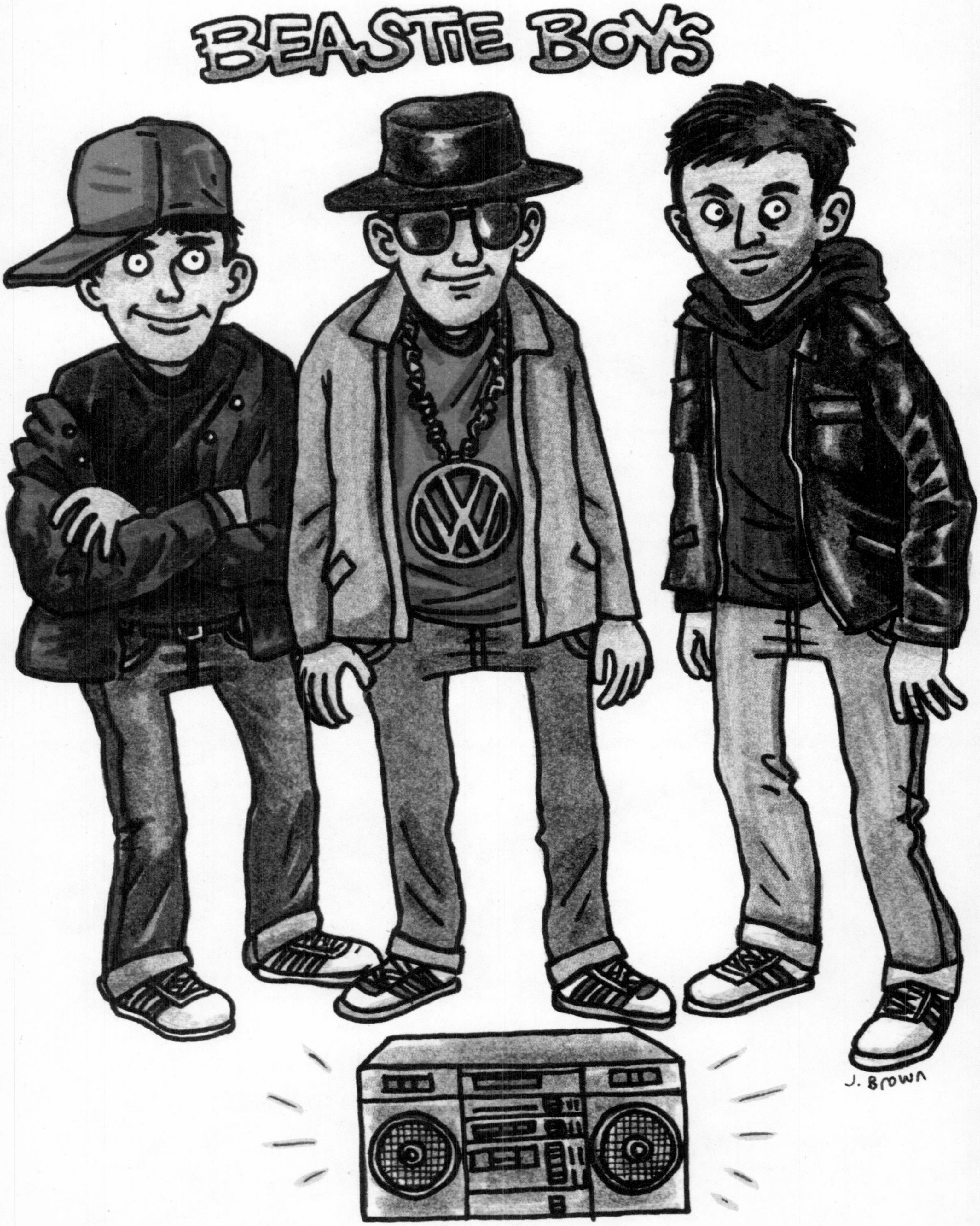
BEASTIE BOYS
J. BROWN

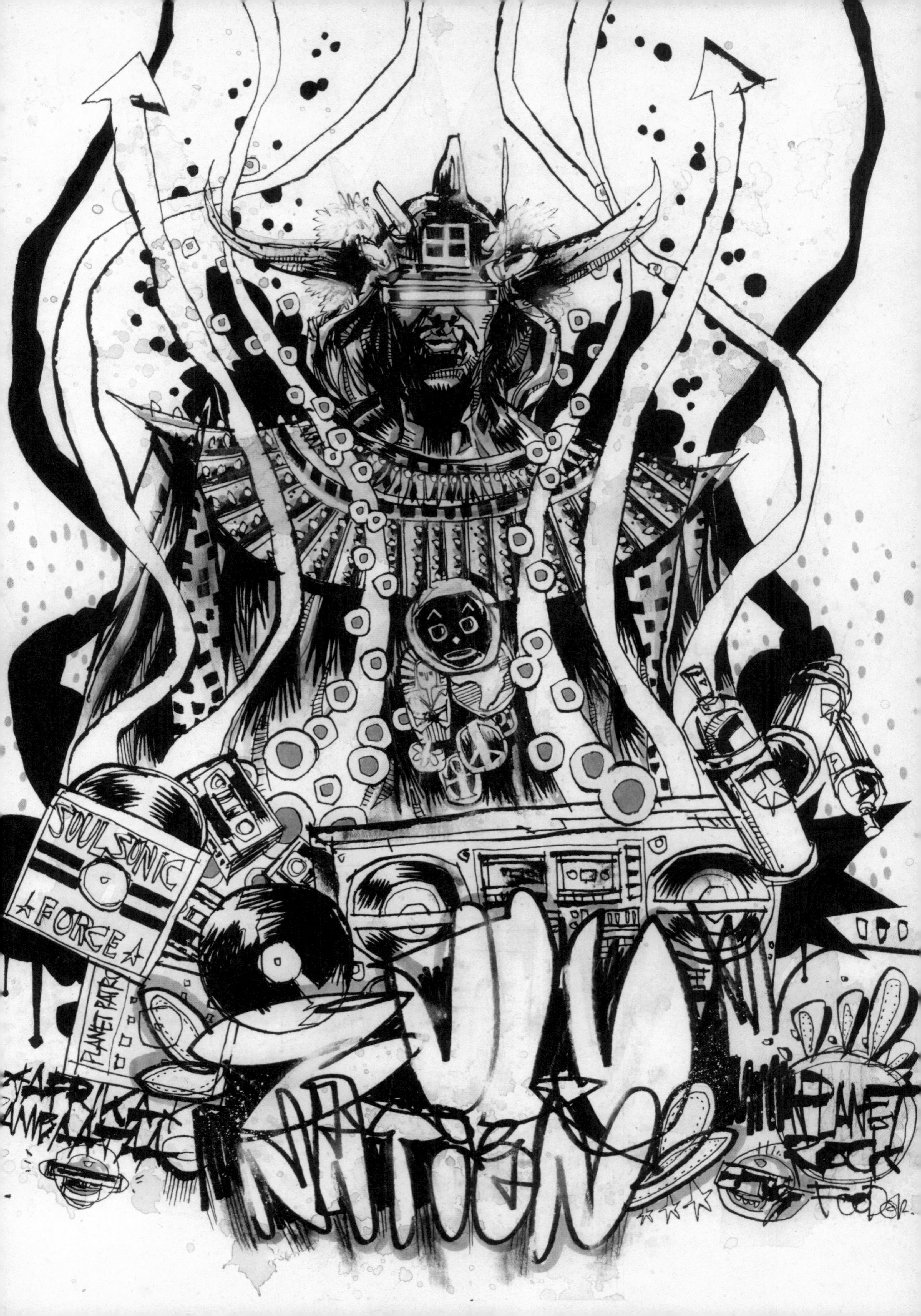
SOUL SONIC
FORCE

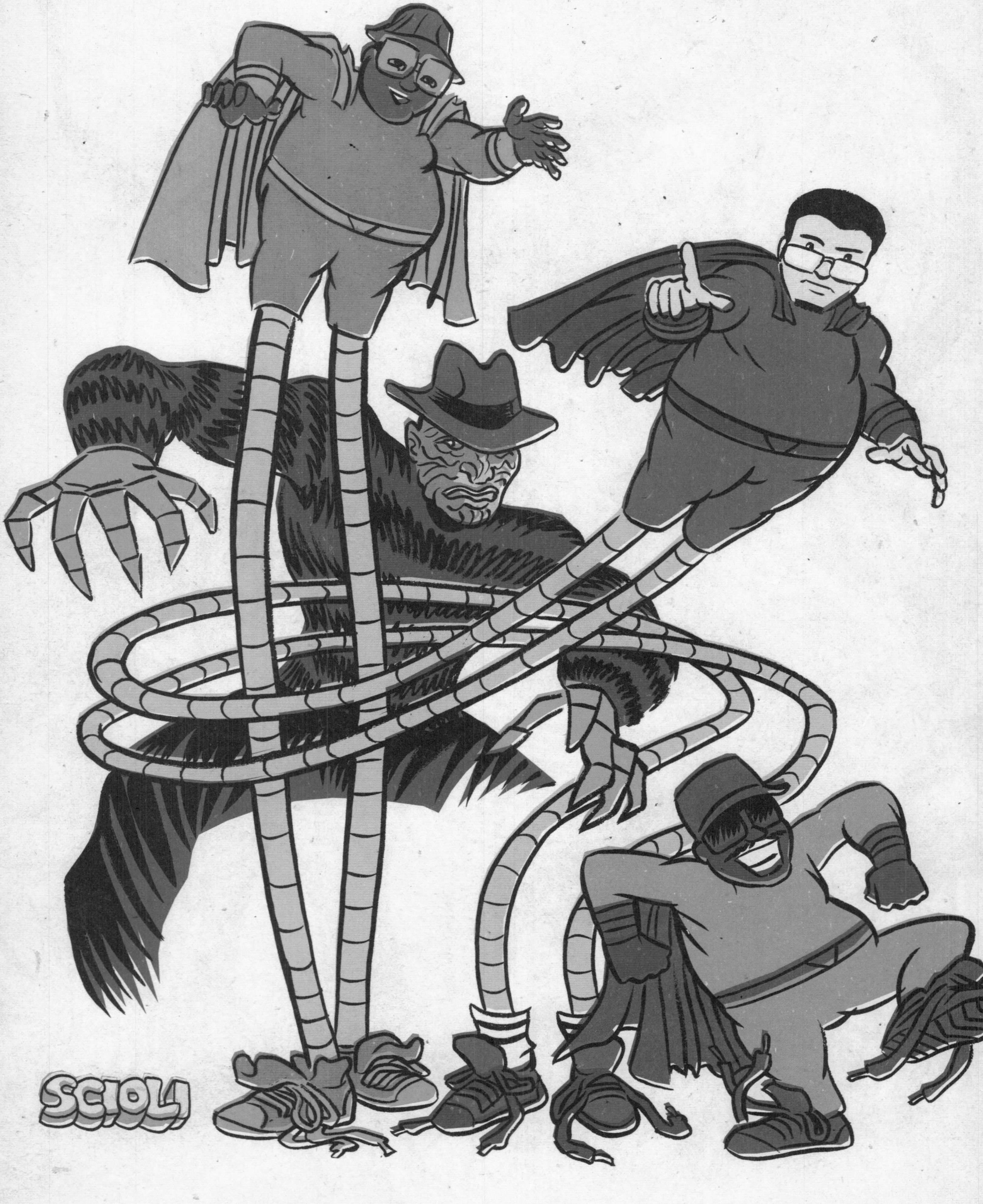
SCIOLI

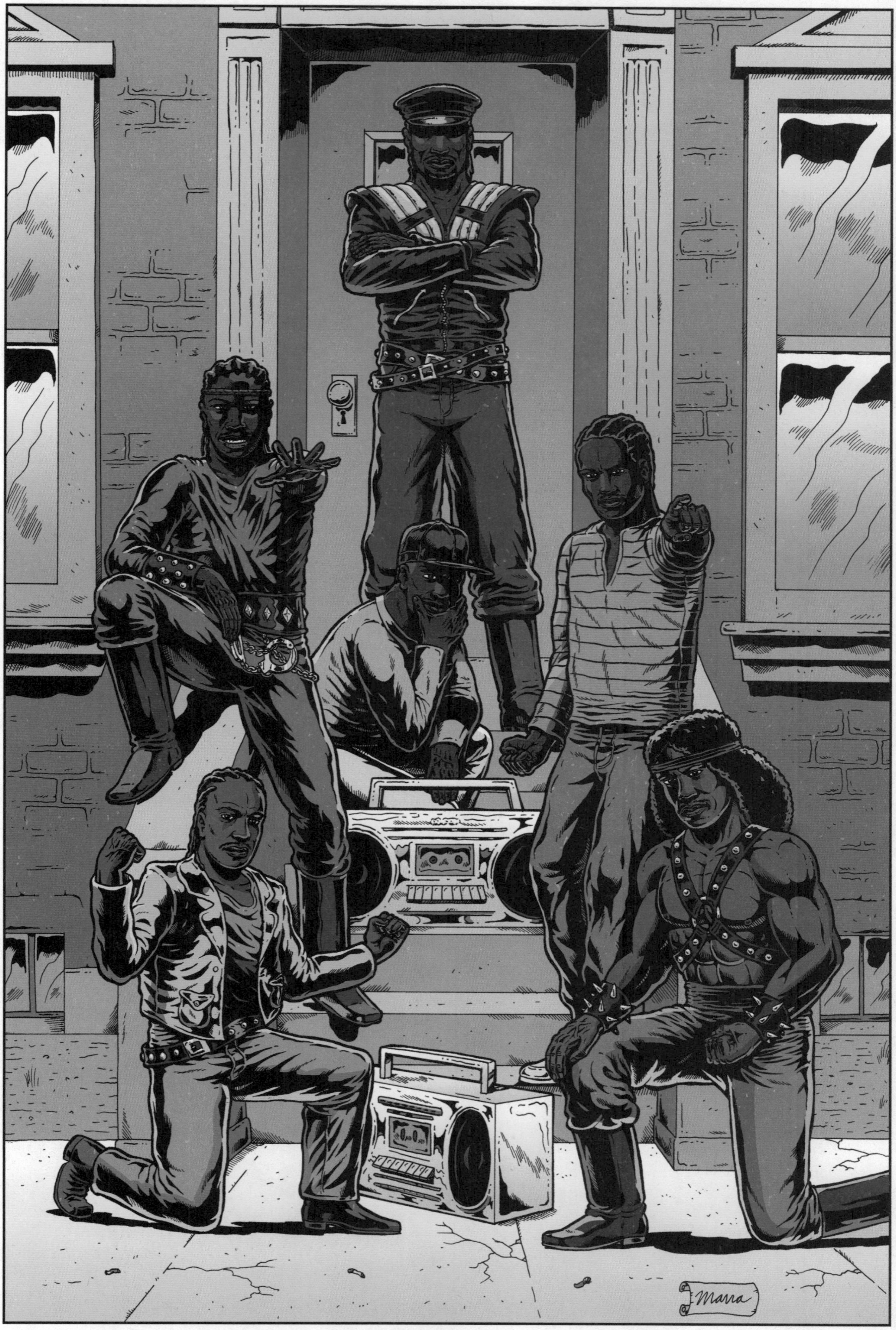
Marra

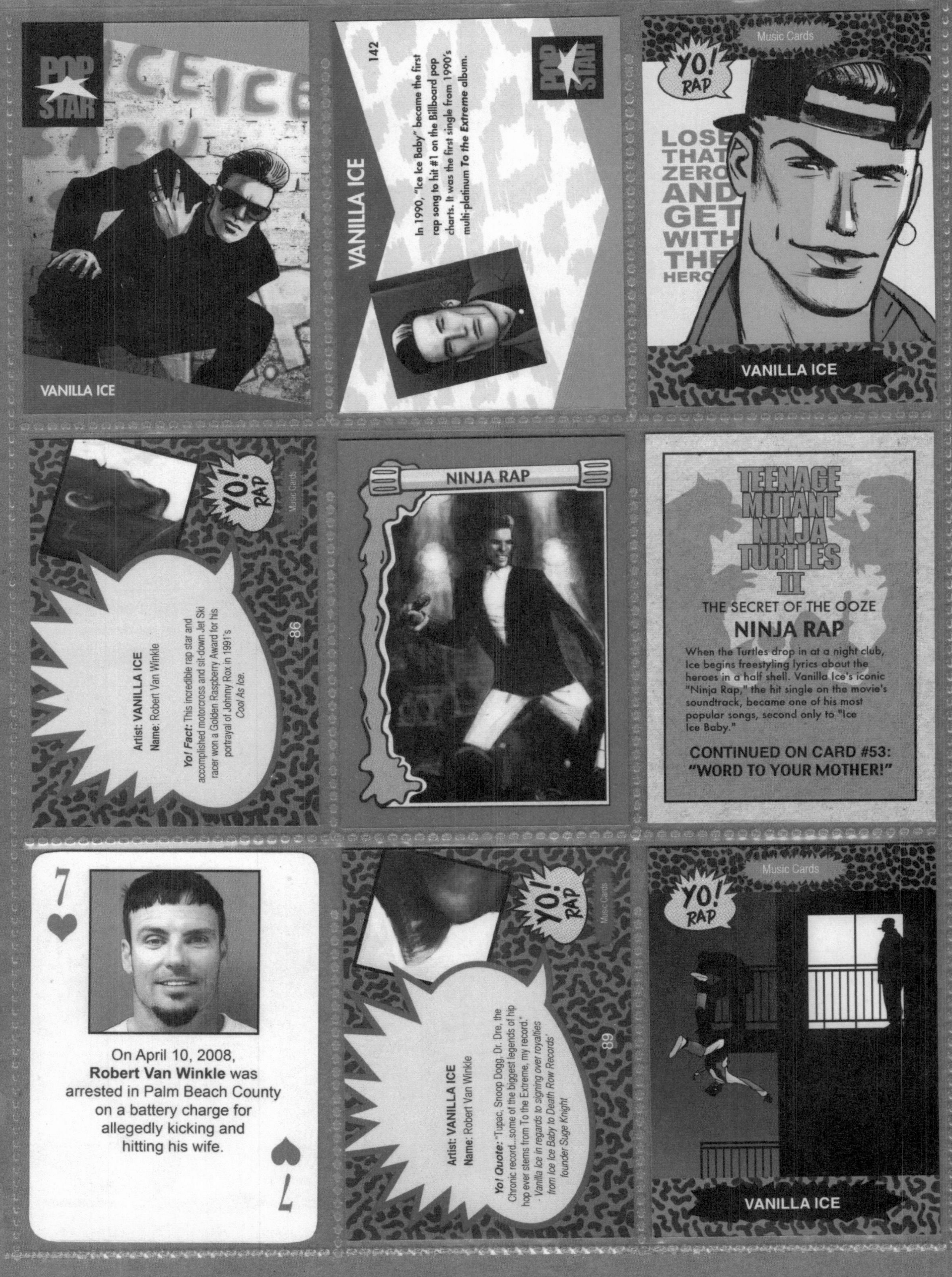
POP STAR
VANILLA ICE
142
POP STAR
VANILLA ICE
In 1990, "Ice Ice Baby" became the first rap song to hit #1 on the Billboard pop charts. It was the first single from 1990's multi-platinum To the Extreme album.
Music Cards
YO! RAP
LOSE THAT ZERO AND GET WITH THE HERO
VANILLA ICE
YO! RAP
Music Cards
86
Artist: VANILLA ICE
Name: Robert Van Winkle
Yo! Fact: This incredible rap star and accomplished motorcross and sit-down Jet Ski racer won a Golden Raspberry Award for his portrayal of Johnny Rox in 1991's Cool As Ice.
NINJA RAP
TEENAGE MUTANT NINJA TURTLES II
THE SECRET OF THE OOZE
NINJA RAP
When the Turtles drop in at a night club, Ice begins freestyling lyrics about the heroes in a half shell. Vanilla Ice's iconic "Ninja Rap," the hit single on the movie's soundtrack, became one of his most popular songs, second only to "Ice Ice Baby."
CONTINUED ON CARD #53: "WORD TO YOUR MOTHER!"
7
On April 10, 2008, Robert Van Winkle was arrested in Palm Beach County on a battery charge for allegedly kicking and hitting his wife.
7
YO! RAP
Music Cards
89
Artist: VANILLA ICE
Name: Robert Van Winkle
Yo! Quote: "Tupac, Snoop Dogg, Dr. Dre, the Chronic record...some of the biggest legends of hip hop ever stems from To the Extreme, my record."
- Vanilla Ice in regards to signing over royalties from Ice Ice Baby to Death Row Records' founder Suge Knight
Music Cards
YO! RAP
VANILLA ICE

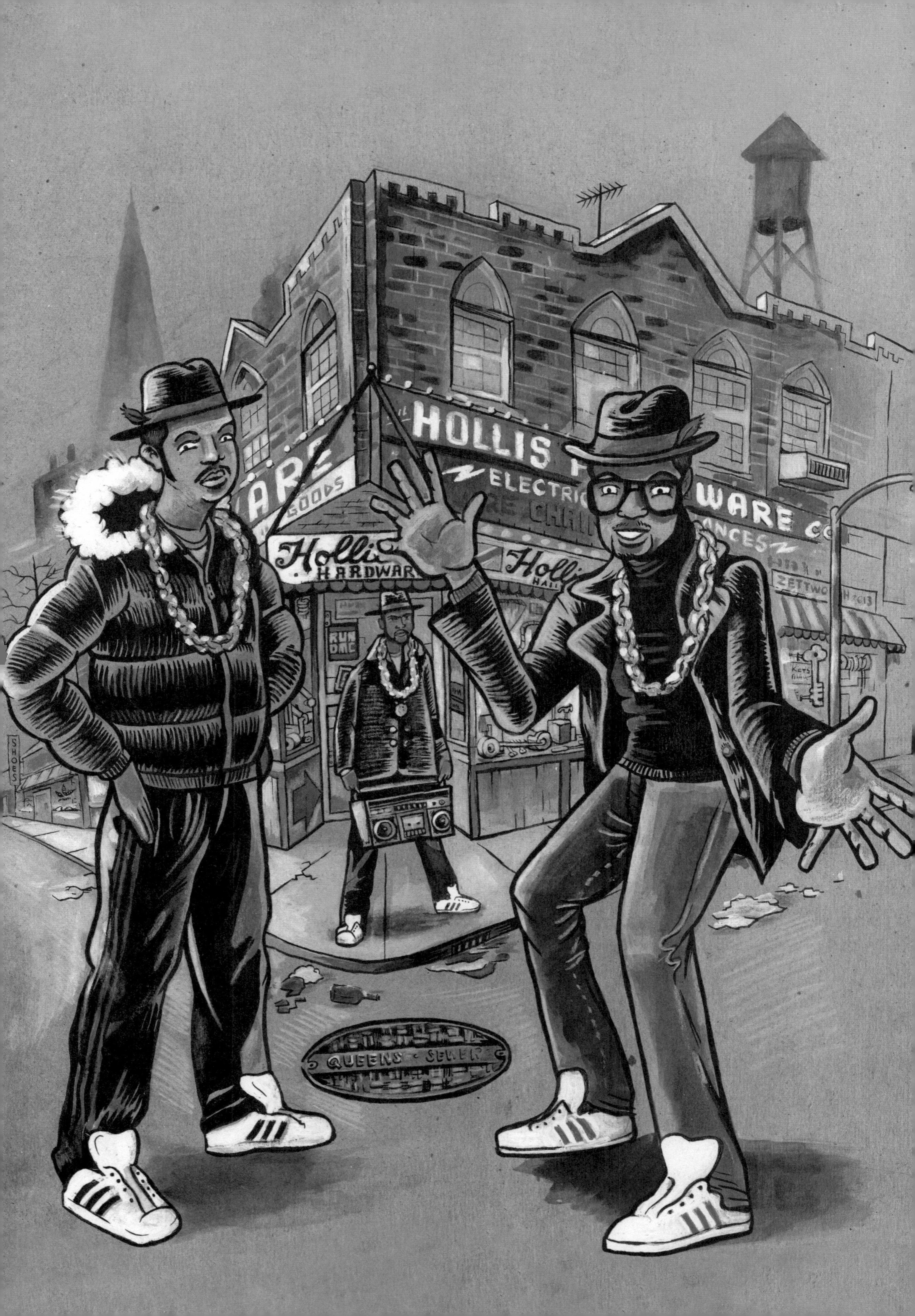
HOLLIS
ELECTRIC
WARE
GOODS
Holli
HARDWAR
RUN DMC
SHOES
QUEENS · SEWER

ERIC B. + RAKIM
"LYRICS OF FURY"

John Porcellino
2013

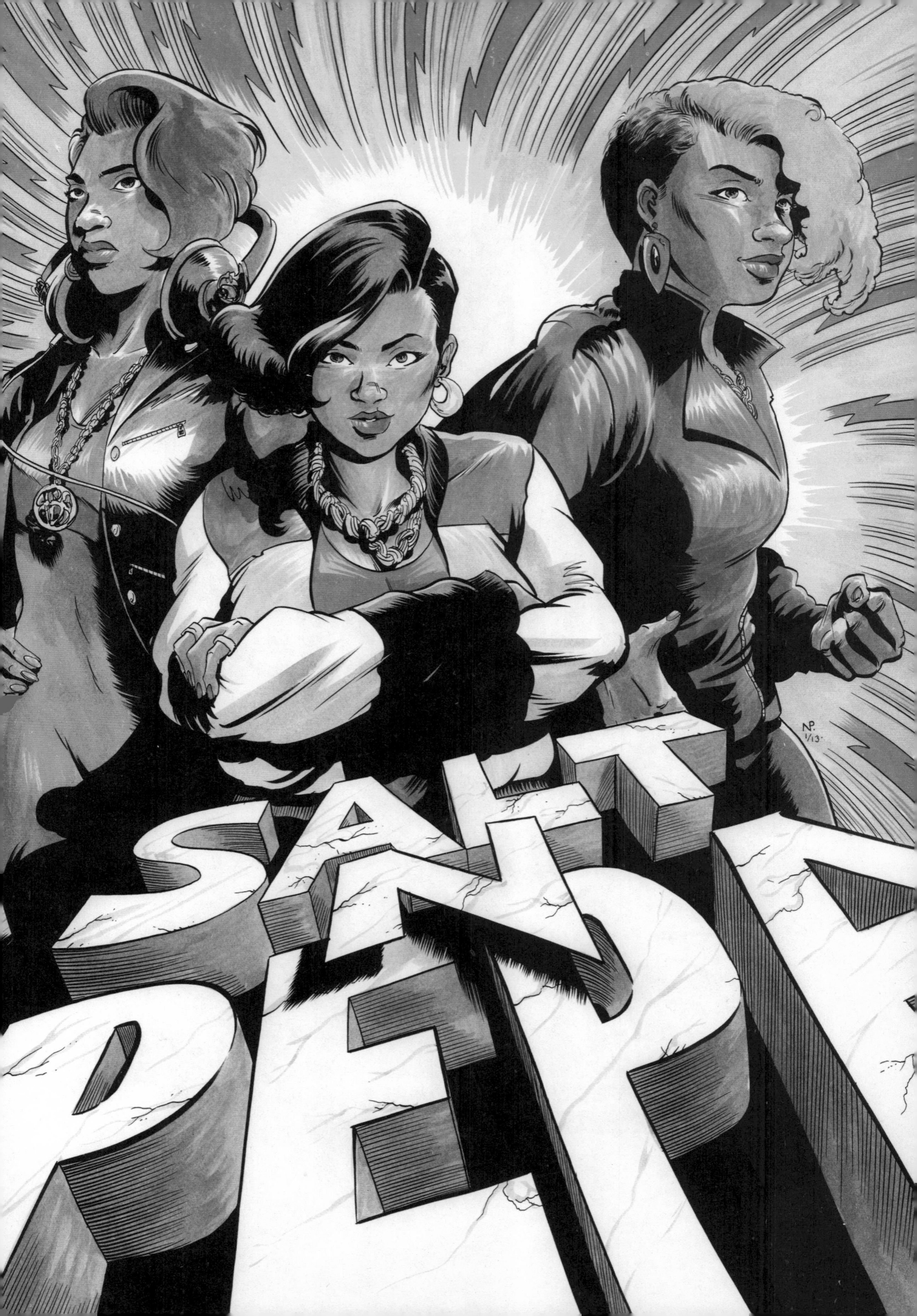

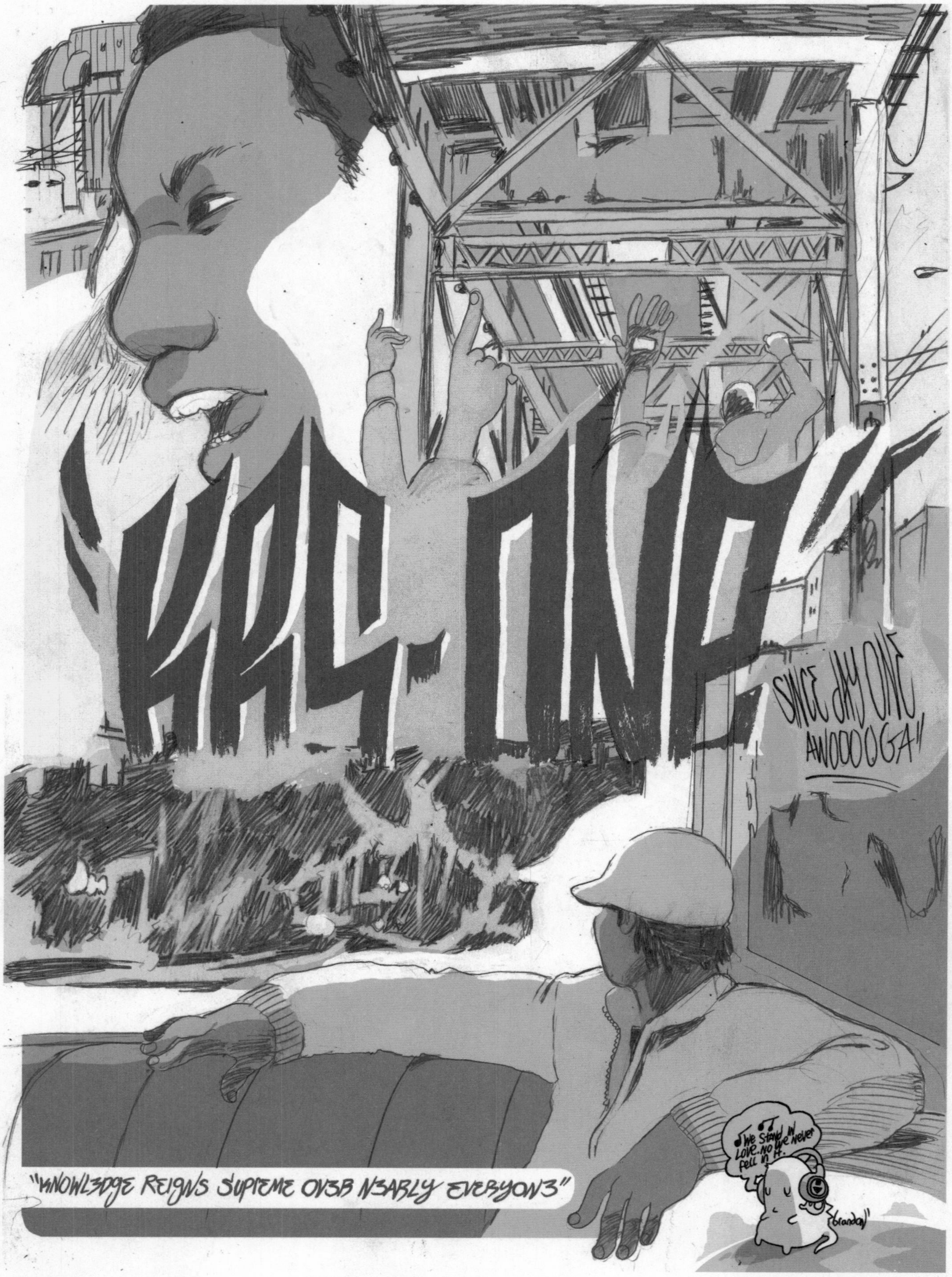
KRS-ONE
SINCE DAY ONE AWOOOOGA"
We stand in love. No we never fell in it.
"KNOWL3DGE REIGNS SUPREME OV3R N3ARLY EVERYON3"

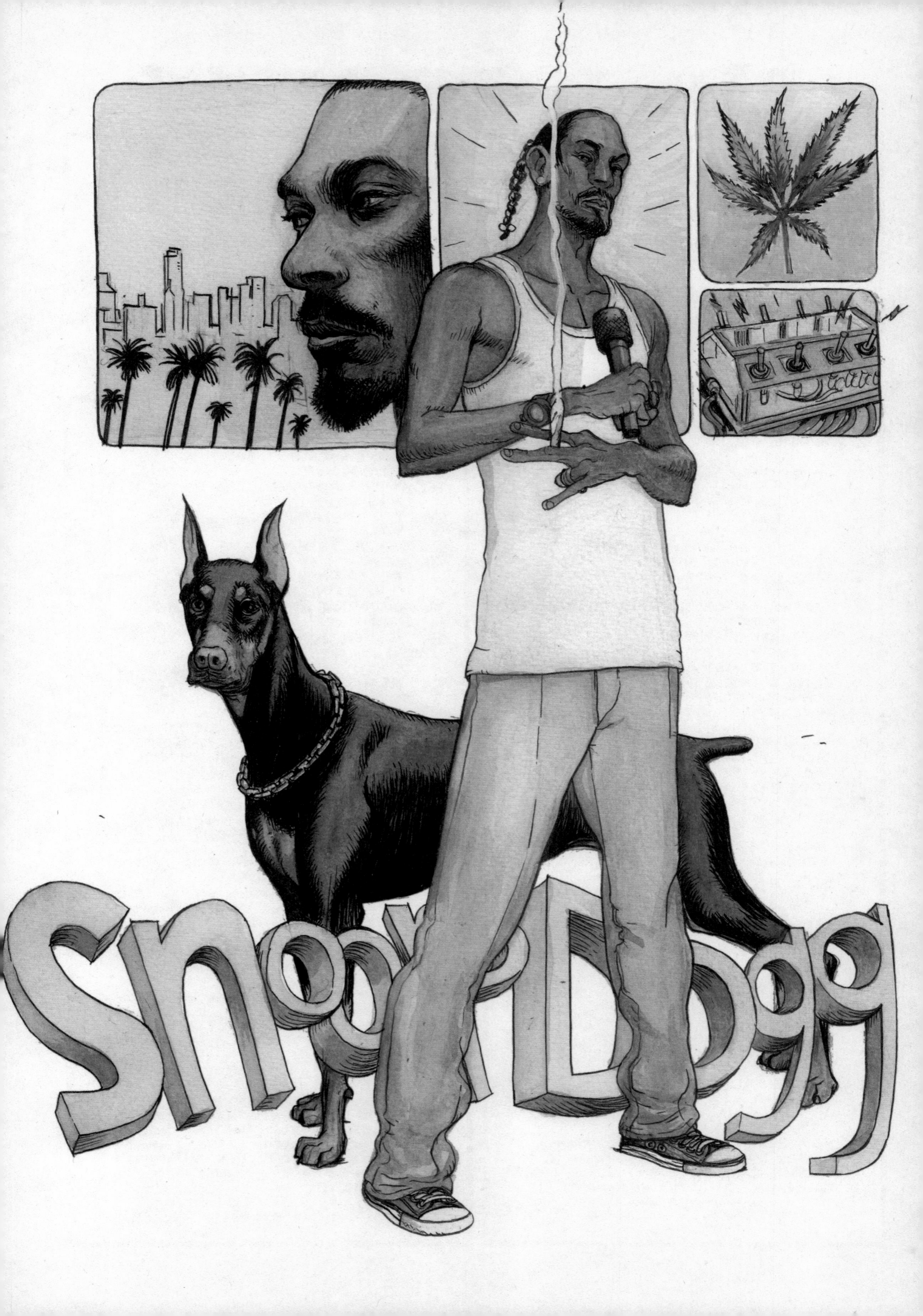
Snoop Dogg

BIBLIOGRAPHY

CHANG, JEFF. **CAN'T STOP, WON'T STOP: A HISTORY OF THE HIP HOP GENERATION.** NEW YORK, NY: ST. MARTINS, 2005. PRINT

CHARNAS, DAN. **THE BIG PAYBACK: THE HISTORY OF THE BUSINESS OF HIP HOP.** NEW YORK, NY: NEW AMERICAN LIBRARY, 2010. PRINT

FRESH, FREDDY. **FREDDY FRESH PRESENTS THE RAP RECORDS.** SAINT PAUL, MN: NERBY PUB. LLC, 2004. PRINT.

FRICKE, JIM, AND CHARLIE AHEARN. **YES YES Y'ALL: THE EXPERIENCE MUSIC PROJECT ORAL HISTORY OF HIP HOP'S FIRST DECADE.** CAMBRIDGE, MA: DA CAPO, 2002. PRINT

JENKINS, SACHA. **EGO TRIP'S BOOK OF RAP LISTS.** NEW YORK, NY: ST. MARTIN'S GRIFFIN, 1999. PRINT

SIMMONS, RUSSELL AND NELSON GEORGE. **LIFE AND DEF: SEX, DRUGS, MONEY, AND GOD.** NEW YORK, NY: CROWN, 2001. PRINT.

DISCOGRAPHY

1. "KING TIM III": FATBACK BAND (SPRING)
2. "RAPPER'S DELIGHT": SUGARHILL GANG (SUGAR HILL)
3. "RHYMIN' AND RAPPIN'": PAULETTE & TANYA WINLEY (WINLEY)
4. "SPOONIN' RAP": SPOONIE GEE (SOUND OF NEW YORK)
5. "WE RAP MORE MELLOW": THE YOUNGER GENERATION [GRANDMASTER FLASH & THE FURIOUS FIVE] (BRASS)
6. "CHRISTMAS RAPPIN'": KURTIS BLOW (MERCURY)
7. "RAPPIN' AND ROCKIN' THE HOUSE": FUNKY 4+1 (ENJOY)
8. "SUPERAPPIN'": GRANDMASTER FLASH AND THE FURIOUS FIVE (ENJOY)
9. "TO THE BEAT, Y'ALL": LADY B (TEC)
10. "FUNK YOU UP": SEQUENCE (SUGAR HILL)
11. "HIGH POWER RAP": DISCO DAVE AND THE FORCE OF THE FIVE MC'S [CRASH CREW] (MIKE AND DAVE)
12. "THE BREAKS": KURTIS BLOW (MERCURY)
13. "NEW RAP LANGUAGE": THE TREACHEROUS THREE (ENJOY)
14. "LOVE RAP": SPOONIE GEE (ENJOY)
15. "THAT'S THE JOINT": FUNKY FOUR+1 (SUGAR HILL)
16. "MONSTER JAM": SEQUENCE FEATURING SPOONIE GEE (SUGAR HILL)
17. "FEEL THE HEARTBEAT": TREACHEROUS THREE (ENJOY)
18. "PUT THE BOOGIE IN YOUR BODY": TREACHEROUS THREE (ENJOY)
19. "THE BODY ROCK": TREACHEROUS THREE (ENJOY)
20. "AT THE PARTY": TREACHEROUS THREE (ENJOY)
21. "CAN I GET A SOUL CLAP, FRESH OUT THE PACK": GRAND WIZARD THEODORE & THE FANTASTIC ROMANTIC FIVE (SOUL WAX)
22. "FREEDOM": GRANDMASTER FLASH AND THE FURIOUS FIVE (SUGAR HILL)
23. "SHOCK, SHOCK THE HOUSE": DJ HOLLYWOOD (EPIC)
24. "RAPPIN' ALL OVER": THE YOUNGER GENERATION (BRASS)
25. "LET'S ROCK": HARLEM WORLD CREW (TAYSTER)
26. "RAPPERS CONVENTION": HARLEM WORLD CREW (TAYSTER)
27. "YOUNG LADIES": LONNIE LOVE (NIA)
28. "ZULU NATION THROWDOWN VOL 1": AFRIKA BAMBAATAA AND THE COSMIC FORCE (WINLEY)
29. "ZULU NATION THROWDOWN VOL. 2": AFRIKA BAMBAATAA AND THE SOUL SONIC FORCE (WINLEY)
30. "VICIOUS RAP": TANYA WINLEY (WINLEY)
31. "ADVENTURES OF SUPER RHYME": JIMMY SPICER (DAZZ)
32. "8TH WONDER": SUGARHILL GANG (SUGAR HILL)
33. "RAPPIN' WITH MR. MAGIC": MR. MAGIC (MAGIC)
34. "GET UP (AND GO TO SCHOOL)": POOKEY BLOW (TRI-STATE)
35. "BIG APPLE RAPPIN'": SPYDER D (NEWTROIT)
36. "HOW WE GONNA MAKE THE BLACK NATION RISE": BROTHER D AND THE COLLECTIVE EFFORT (CLAPPERS)
37. "WE WANT TO ROCK": CRASH CREW (SUGAR HILL)
38. "RAPTURE": BLONDIE (CHRYSALIS)
39. "THE ADVENTURES OF GRANDMASTER FLASH ON THE WHEELS OF STEEL": GRANDMASTER FLASH AND THE FURIOUS FIVE (SUGAR HILL)
40. "JAZZY SENSATION": AFRIKA BAMBAATAA AND THE JAZZY FIVE (TOMMY BOY)

BREAKS & BEATS

1. "APACHE": INCREDIBLE BONGO BAND (PRIDE)
2. "BRA": CYMANDE (JANUS)
3. "GOOD TIMES": CHIC (ATLANTIC)
4. "WALK THIS WAY": AEROSMITH (COLUMBIA)
5. "IT'S JUST BEGUN": JIMMY CASTOR (RCA)
6. "THE CHAMP": THE MOHAWKS (PAMA)
7. "FUNKY DRUMMER": JAMES BROWN (KING)
8. "TAKE ME TO THE MARDI GRAS": BOB JAMES (CTI)
9. "TRAMP": OTIS REDDING AND CARLA THOMAS (STAX)
10. "SCORPIO": DENNIS COFFEY (SUSSEX)
11. "BONGO ROCK '73": INCREDIBLE BONGO BAND (PRIDE)
12. "GET ON THE GOOD FOOT": JAMES BROWN (POLYDOR)
13. "SCRATCHIN'": MAGIC DISCO MACHINE (MOTOWN)
14. "I KNOW YOU GOT SOUL": BOBBY BIRD (KING)
15. "GET UP AND DANCE": FREEDOM (MALACO)
16. "AIN'T NO HALF STEPPIN'": HEAT WAVE (GTO)
17. "THE MEXICAN": BABE RUTH (HARVEST)
18. "LISTEN TO ME": BABY HUEY (CURTOM)
19. "MELTING POT": BOOKER T AND THE M.G'S (STAX)
20. "MARY MARY": THE MONKEES (COLGEMS)

FUNKY INDEX

SITTING AROUND ALL DAY DRAWING AND LISTENING TO MUSIC (and Howard Stern), I OFTEN THINK ABOUT THE MANY SIMILARITIES BETWEEN COMICS AND RAP MUSIC (a division of Hip Hop culture). THE FOLLOWING COULD ALL BE FORCED CORRELATIONS BECAUSE OF MY BLINDING LOVE OF THE TWO, I ADMIT. WHATEVER!

THE HIP HOP/COMIC BOOK CONNECTION

ONE THING THAT SPRINGS TO MIND IS THAT BOTH THE PHYSICAL COMIC BOOK AND HIP HOP ARE DISTINCTLY AMERICAN INVENTIONS. BOTH FROM NEW YORK, NO LESS!

THEY ALSO WERE CULTURAL BASTARD CHILDREN THAT GAINED INCREASED RESPECT OVER TIME.

SAY WHAT YOU WILL ABOUT **TIME** MAGAZINE... THEY PUT **WATCHMEN** ON THE SAME LIST AS **ULYSSES**...

...AND **PAID IN FULL** ON THE SAME LIST AS **ABBEY ROAD**!

URBAN LANDSCAPES! THIS ALWAYS APPEALED TO ME BECAUSE OF WHERE I WAS RAISED. THE BACKGROUNDS IN SUPERHERO COMICS FELT LIKE HOME, AND RAPPERS ARTICULATED WHAT WAS HAPPENING AROUND ME BETTER THAN MY PARENTS COULD.

NICE FLOW, DIONTE!

WORD!

ROMAR'S NEXT IN THE CYPHER.

DIP DIP DIVE, SO SOCIALIZE...

BOMP BOMP BOMP BOMP

BEAT BOXING

FIRST APPEARANCES!

I SAVED UP $9 WORTH OF LUNCH MONEY SO THAT I COULD OWN **NEW MUTANTS #87**, THE FIRST FULL APPEARANCE OF **CABLE**, DRAWN BY MY HERO, ROB LIEFELD.

RAPPERS RARELY WOULD DEBUT ON THEIR OWN RECORDS. IT'S FUN TO DIG UP THEIR EARLIEST EFFORTS. THERE ARE SOME SKELETONS TO UNEARTH IF YOU LOOK HARD ENOUGH...

CALLING DR. DRE TO SUR-JAH-REE!

WIK WIK

ALTER EGOS!!

JOSEPH SIMMONS

DARRYL McDANIELS

DANIEL DUMILE

RICHARD WALTERS

ANDY

CARLTON D. RIDENHOUR

NORMAN ROGERS

WILLIAM DRAYTON

COOL COSTUMES!!

EPIC BATTLES!

BAW WITTA BAW, DANG D-DANG DIGGY...

BUSY B VS. KOOL MOE DEE

BUSY BEE, I DON'T MEAN TO BE **BOLD**, BUT PUT THAT "BAW DITTY BAW" BULL- SHIT ON **HOLD**...

LL COOL J VS. KOOL MOE DEE

ICONIC GROUPS

TEAM-UPS AND COLLABORATIONS

HYPED-UP CROSSOVERS!

HUGE THANKS TO "TANTALIZING" TOM SCIOLI, FOR DRAWING THE SUPERHERO BATTLE PANELS. FOR MORE OF HIS WORK: WWW.AMBARB.COM

ABOUT THE AUTHOR

ED PISKOR (1982) HAS MASTERFULLY CONCOCTED
A SCHEME TO INDULGE IN HIS OBSESSIONS,
GUILT-FREE, BY MAKING COMICS INVOLVING
HIS FAVORITE SUBJECTS. **WIZZYWIG** (TOP
SHELF, 2012) WAS THE RESULT OF HIS INTEREST
IN COMPUTER HACKING AND SOCIAL ENGINEERING.
NOW ILLUSTRATING HIS LOVE OF RAP MUSIC AND
HIP HOP CULTURE, HE HOPES TO CREATE MORE
VOLUMES OF THE **HIP HOP FAMILY TREE**.

HE'S CONTINUING THIS SAGA ONLINE AT
BOINGBOING.NET EACH WEEK, UNLESS
SOME BIG-TIME SHIT WENT DOWN.

THAT SAID, YOU MIGHT WANT TO CONTACT ED
AND SEE WHAT THE HELL'S UP.

WWW.EDPISKOR.COM

EMAIL: WIMPYRUTHERFORD@GMAIL.COM
TWITTER: @EDPISKOR

ORIGINAL ART IS AVAILABLE FOR PURCHASE.
EMAIL ED FOR RATES.

SPOONIE GEE

KOOL MOE DEE

L.A. SUNSHINE

SPECIAL K

T LA ROCK

TED DEMME

CORDIE-O

MEAN GENE

WATERBED KEV

MASTER ROB

CHERYL THE PEARL

ANGIE B.

BLONDY

DJ CHARLIE CHASE

GLENN O'BRIEN

RICK RUBIN

JIMMY SPICER

SPYDER D

CARLTON D. RIDENHOUR

CHARLIE AHEARN

DISCO DAVE

MIXMASTER MIKE

DR. JECKYLL

MR. HYDE

DJ JAZZY JAY